A GARDENER'S GUIDE TO

FLOWERING HOUSEPLANTS

How to enjoy year-round colour in your home
Featuring 150 plants

Aechmea chantinii

Catharanthus roseus

A GARDENER'S GUIDE TO

FLOWERING HOUSEPLANTS

How to enjoy year-round colour in your home
Featuring 150 plants

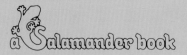

William Davidson

a Salamander book

Published by Salamander Books Limited
LONDON

A Salamander Book

Published by Salamander Books Ltd.,
52 Bedford Row,
London WC1R 4LR.

ISBN 0 86101 397 2

Distributed by
Hodder and Stoughton Services,
PO Box 6, Mill Road, Dunton Green,
Sevenoaks, Kent TN13 2XX.

Contents

The plants are arranged in alphabetical order of Latin name.
Page numbers in **bold** refer to text entries; those in *italics* refer to photographs.

Abutilon hybrids	**17**	*8*
Acacia armata	**17**	*8*
Acalypha hispida	**18**	*9*
Achimenes hybrids	**18**	*10*
Adenium obesum	**19**	*11*
Aechmea chantinii	**19**	*10*
Aechmea fasciata	**20**	
Aeschynanthus lobbianus	**20**	*11*
Allamanda cathartica	**21**	
Alpinia purpurata	**21**	*13*
Angraecum eburneum	**22**	*13*
Anguloa clowesii	**22**	*12*
Anthurium andreanum	**23**	*15*
Anthurium scherzerianum	**23**	
Aphelandra squarrosa	**24**	*14*
Ardisia crispa/crenata	**24**	*14*
Astrophytum asterias	**25**	
Azalea indica	**25**	*16*
Begonia boweri	**26**	*16*
Begonia 'Fireglow'	**26**	
Begonia 'Orange Rubra'	**27**	*33*
Begonia semperflorens	**27**	*33*
Beloperone guttata	**28**	
Billbergia pyramidalis	**28**	*34*
Bougainvillea	**29**	*35*
Bouvardia domestica	**29**	
Brassavola nodosa	**30**	*34*
Browallia speciosa	**30**	*36*
Calanthe vestita	**31**	*36*
Calceolaria hybrids	**31**	
Callistemon citrinus	**32**	*37*
Camellia japonica	**32**	*37*
Campanula isophylla	**49**	
Capsicum annuum	**49**	*38*
Catharanthus roseus	**50**	*39*
Cattleya hybrids	**50**	*38*
Celosia argentea	**51**	*40*
Chamaecereus silvestrii	**51**	
Chrysanthemum	**52**	
Cineraria cruenta	**52**	
Citrus mitis	**53**	*41*
Clerodendrum thomsoniae	**53**	
Clivia miniata	**54**	*43*
Coelogyne cristata	**54**	
Coelogyne ochracea	**55**	*42*
Columnea banksii	**55**	
Columnea microphylla	**56**	*41*
Crassula falcata	**56**	
Crocus	**57**	*42*
Crossandra infundibuliformis	**57**	
Cuphea ignea	**58**	*44*
Cyclamen persicum	**58**	*45*
Cymbidium hybrids	**59**	*44*
Dendrobium Gatton Sunray	**59**	*47*
Dipladenia splendens 'Rosea'	**60**	
Echeveria 'Doris Taylor'	**60**	*46*
Echinocereus baileyi	**61**	
Echinopsis hybrids	**61**	
Encyclia cochleata	**62**	*47*
Epiphyllum	**62**	
Episcia cupreata	**63**	*48*
Episcia dianthiflora	**63**	*48*
Erica	**64**	
Eucharis grandiflora	**64**	*65*
Euphorbia fulgens	**81**	
Euphorbia milii	**81**	*67*
Euphorbia pulcherrima	**82**	*66/7*
Exacum affine	**82**	*66*
Freesia	**83**	*69*
Fuchsia	**83**	*68*
Gardenia jasminoides	**84**	*68*
Gloriosa rothschildiana	**84**	*71*
Guzmania lingulata	**85**	*71*
Gymnocalycium mihanovichi 'Hibotan'	**85**	*70*
Haemanthus katharinae	**86**	*73*
Hedychium gardnerianum	**86**	
Heliconia angustifolia	**87**	*72*
Heliotropium hybrids	**87**	*72*

Credits

Author: William Davidson is involved with all aspects of houseplants, and has been employed by Rochfords, Europe's leading growers, for most of his working life. His interests encompass growing, exhibiting, writing, consultancy, lecturing, as well as radio and television programmes. He is the author of many successful books on houseplants.

Consultant: Sue Minter, a qualified horiticulturalist, has edited and contributed to several plant books.

Editor: Geoff Rogers

Line drawings: Tyler/Camoccio Design Consultants

Photographs: A full list of credits is given on page 160.
Colour reproductions: Scansets Ltd., Middlesex, England. Bantam Litho Ltd., Essex, England.
Monochrome: Tenreck, London, England.
Filmset: SX Composing Ltd., Essex, England.

Printed in Belgium by Henri Proost & Cie, Turnhout.

Hibiscus rosa-sinensis	**88**	*74*
Hippeastrum hybrids	**88**	
Hoya australis	**89**	*75*
Hoya bella	**89**	*75*
Hoya carnosa	**90**	
Hyacinthus orientalis	**90**	*74*
Hydrangea macrophylla	**91**	*77*
Hypocyrta glabra	**91**	
Impatiens wallerana	**92**	
Ixia hybrids	**92**	*78*
Ixora coccinea	**93**	*79*
Jacobinia carnea	**93**	*79*
Jasminum polyanthum	**94**	
Kalanchoe blossfeldiana	**94**	
Kalanchoe pumila	**95**	*79*
Kohleria amabilis	**95**	*80*
Laelia anceps	**96**	*97*
Lantana camara	**96**	*98*
Lapageria rosea	**113**	*99*
Lilium auratum	**113**	*98*
Lithops	**114**	
Lobivia aurea	**114**	*100*
Lycaste aromatica	**115**	*101*
Mammillaria zeilmanniana	**115**	*101*
Manettia bicolor	**116**	
Masdevallia coccinea	**116**	*102*
Medinilla magnifica	**117**	*103*
Miltonia Peach Blossom	**117**	*103*
Miltonia roezlii	**118**	*104*
Narcissus tazetta	**118**	*105*
Nerine bowdenii	**119**	*105*
Nerium oleander	**119**	*104*
Notocactus leninghausii	**120**	*106*
Notocactus ottonis	**120**	*106*
Odontioda	**121**	*107*
Odontoglossum grande	**121**	*109*
Oncidium ornithorhynchum	**122**	
Oncidium papilio	**122**	
Pachystachys lutea	**123**	*108*
Paphiopedilum Maudiae	**123**	
Parodia sanguiniflora	**124**	
Passiflora caerulea	**124**	*108*
Pelargonium	**125**	*110*
Pentas lanceolota	**126**	*112*
Phalaenopsis Hennessy	**126**	*129*
Pleione formosana	**127**	*112*
Primula malacoides	**127**	*129*
Primula obconica	**128**	
Primula vulgaris	**128**	
Punica granatum 'Nana'	**145**	*130*
Rebutia calliantha var. krainziana	**145**	*131*
Rechsteineria cardinalis	**146**	*130*
Rivina humilis	**146**	
Saintpaulia ionantha	**147**	*133*
Schizocentron elegans	**147**	*132*
Schlumbergera 'Buckleyi'	**148**	*132*
Schlumbergera gaertneri	**148**	*134*
Sinningia speciosa	**149**	*135*
Smithiantha cinnabarina	**149**	*134*
Solanum capsicastrum	**150**	*136*
Spathiphyllum 'Mauna Loa'	**150**	*137*
Sprekelia formosissima	**151**	
Stanhopea wardii	**151**	*136*
Stephanotis floribunda	**152**	*141*
Strelitzia reginae	**152**	*139*
Streptocarpus hybrids	**153**	*139*
Thunbergia alata	**153**	*138*
Tillandsia cyanea	**154**	
Trichopilia tortilis	**154**	*141*
Tulipa	**155**	*140*
Vallota speciosa	**155**	*140*
Vanda suavis	**156**	*142*
Veltheimia viridifolia	**156**	
Vriesea splendens	**157**	*142*
Zantedeschia rehmannii	**157**	
Zephyranthes candida	**158**	*143*
Zygopetalum intermedium	**158**	*144*
Index of common names	**159**	
Picture credits	**160**	

Guzmania lingulata 'Minor Orange'

Introduction

There is nothing quite so disappointing as watching a cherished houseplant slowly dying in your care. Despite all your efforts, it never seems to regain the vitality it once enjoyed in the plant shop. Not surprisingly, this experience may persuade you that you will never succeed with any plants in your home. This is regrettable, because with just a little encouragement and the suggestion of a plant more suited to your home conditions, you might well become a successful and even a fanatic houseplant grower.

Whether you are one of life's 'plant refugees' or able to grow a wide range of houseplants with consummate skill, this guide will give you the incentive to try something new. Here is a selection of over 150 flowering houseplants, described with enthusiasm as well as accuracy, that can fill your home with colour all year through. The plants are presented in alphabetical order of Latin name and coded in words (not confusing symbols) according to the amount of light they need, their ideal growing temperature (for the orchids this is a winter night minimum), and a note about moisture and/or feeding (or annual growth cycle for the orchids). Clear instructions on the best way to grow each plant are followed by a special tip to encourage flowering.

Each plant is illustrated by a clear line drawing and 120 of the plants are shown in beautiful colour photographs. Text and photographs are cross-referenced throughout (24▸) and an index of common names completes the book.

Above: **Abutilon 'Boule de Neige'**
Well known for their paper-thin orange, yellow or red flowers, abutilons are decorative plants where a vertical accent is necessary. Do stake plants so they do not become unwieldy. 17▸

Left: **Acacia armata**
Grown more outdoors than indoors, this beautiful yellow flowering plant is a happy choice if you have space for it. Flowers appear in early spring and assure colour at the window. 17▸

Right: **Acalypha hispida**
The long chenillelike red catkins make A. hispida a popular houseplant. The large leaves are decorative as well, and when young a fine plant for limited space. 18▸

Left: **Achimenes hybrids 'Paul Arnold'**
Dozens of attractive varieties come from this large gesneriad group, and all offer a wealth of colourful flowers for summer show. 18▸

Below left: **Aechmea chantinii**
Called the 'Queen of the Bromeliads'. A. chantinii has handsome broad leaves, rosette growth and an inflorescence that seems artificial, it is so vividly coloured. Bracts last for months. 19▸

Right: **Adenium obesum 'Multiflorum'**
An extraordinary succulent with rosettes of leaves and large white, crimson-edged flowers. The stems eventually become woody trunks of a sculpturesque form. 19▸

Below: **Aeschynanthus lobbianus**
Brilliant red flowers in tubular 'lipstick cases' adorn this plant in midsummer – a mature specimen may have over 50 flowers. The plant has pendent growth and is best grown in a basket container. 20▸

Left: **Anguloa clowesii**
This yellow tulip orchid is aptly named. Its fragrant blooms cluster at the base of the plant, but are never hidden from view because the leaves are upright. 22▸

Right: **Angraecum eburneum**
Large white to pale green crystalline flowers in winter make this orchid highly desirable for indoor accent, and the evergreen straplike leaves are attractive as well. 22▸

Below: **Alpinia purpurata**
A fine ginger plant – though somewhat large – with dense clusters of red bracts; an excellent touch of tropical atmosphere for a spacious window. 21▸

Above: **Aphelandra squarrosa 'Louisae'**
This fine houseplant from South America has stellar yellow flowers – a brilliant display at any window. A good plant for limited space. 24▸

Left: **Ardisia crispa/crenata**
An ardisia covered with red berries makes a fine winter gift. Leaves are dark green and handsome. This plant from the East Indies is always welcome in window gardens. 24▸

Right: **Anthurium andreanum**
An exotic anthurium from Central America, with its glossy green leaves this is a glamorous subject for a shady part of the indoor garden. It bears large flower spathes throughout the summer, and comes in white or shades of pink and red. 23▸

Above: **Begonia boweri**
Long a favourite, the eyelash begonia has spectacular foliage and white or pale pink flowers that are a delight throughout summer and autumn months of the year. 26▸

Left: **Azalea indica**
Here is a plant that can brighten any autumn day. A compact shrub, it can be in flower for many weeks. 25▸

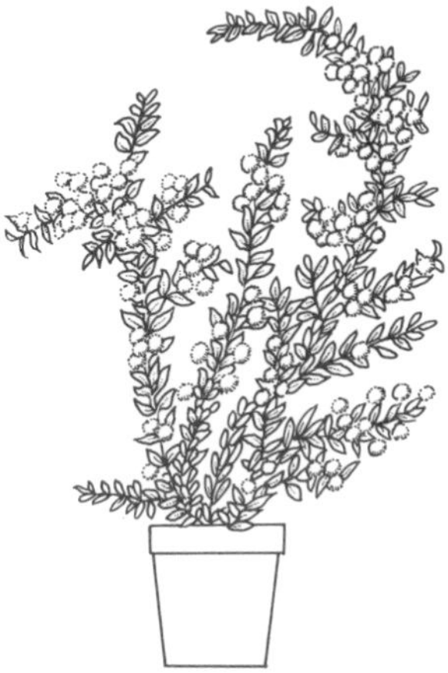

Abutilon hybrids

(Bellflower; Flowering maple)

- **Good light**
- **Temp: 10-18°C (50-65°F)**
- **Keep moist and fed**

There are numerous varieties, with pendulous bell-shaped flowers in a range of colours, and some have colourful foliage. Many of the abutilons are worthy of a place in the houseplant collection for their foliage alone.

Most are of vigorous habit, and capable of attaining a height of some 1.8m (6ft) with their roots confined to a pot of about 18cm (7in) in diameter. However, pruning of over-vigorous growth presents no problem and can be done at almost any time of the year. Firm top sections of stems will not be difficult to root in a fresh peat and sand mixture. Feed well when they are established.

Light, airy and cool conditions suit them best, and they will be the better for spending the summer months out of doors in a sheltered position. Use a loam-based potting mixture.

To encourage bloom:
Keep plants in small pots – a 13-15cm (5-6in) pot is ideal. 8▸

Acacia armata

(Kangaroo thorn; Wattle)

- **Good light**
- **Temp: 13-18°C (55-65°F)**
- **Keep moist**

Native to Australia, *A. armata* develops into an attractive shrubby plant that does well in a conservatory, but may in time become too large for smaller rooms. However, pruning of over-vigorous growth can be undertaken in the early part of the year, which is also the best time for potting plants into larger containers. A loam-based mixture is necessary if plants are not to become too soft and lush.

New plants are made by sowing seed in spring, or by taking firm, but not old, cuttings in midsummer. Older material is too woody and less likely to succeed.

The principal attraction of this plant is the yellow flowers, which appear in spring. During the spring and summer, plants require to be fed regularly and watered freely; they need less water and no feeding during the winter months.

To encourage bloom:
Provide bright and airy conditions around the plant. 8▸

Acalypha hispida

(Chenille plant; Foxtails; Red hot cat's tail)

- **Good light**
- **Temp: 13-18°C (55-65°F)**
- **Keep moist and fed**

These striking plants, with their large leaves of mid-green colouring, grow to a height of some 1.8m (6ft) in ideal conditions. Drooping beetroot-red bracts develop from the axils of leaves to create the principal attraction of this fine plant.

The best time to purchase these plants is in the spring when the fresh young ones will get off to a better start. Keep them moist at all times, giving a little less water in winter, and feed well when they are established. When they have filled their existing containers with roots, use a loam-based potting compost to pot the plants on and help to develop them to their full potential.

Keep your acalypha in good light but avoid strong sunlight. Remove the dead bracts regularly and keep a watchful eye for pale leaf discolouration, which is a sign that troublesome red spider mites are present. Treat the undersides of leaves with insecticide promptly.

To encourage bloom:
Provide plenty of water and light. 9▸

Achimenes hybrids

(Cupid's bower; Hot water plant)

- **Good light**
- **Temp: 13-18°C (55-65°F)**
- **Keep moist and fed**

One of those cheap and cheerful plants that will go on flowering throughout the summer, and can be raised from early spring-sown seed, from cuttings, or by peeling off and planting some of the scaly rhizomes. They are fine as conventional pot plants situated in good light on a windowsill or, perhaps more splendidly, as hanging-basket plants growing overhead.

After the flowers and foliage have died down the plants should be allowed to dry out and rest throughout the winter. They can be started into growth again in the spring. At this time the rhizomes can be peeled apart so that more plants are produced. Place the rhizomes in hot water before planting, and they will generally do better.

Keep the plants moist and avoid a very dry atmosphere, which will encourage red spider mites to the detriment of the plant.

To encourage bloom:
Maintain humid, well-lit conditions during the summer. 10▸

Adenium obesum var. multiflorum

(Desert rose; Impala lily)

- **Full sun**
- **Temp: 13-30°C (55-86°F)**
- **Keep almost dry in winter**

Although it is a succulent plant in its native habitat, this adenium cannot produce the massive water-storage stem as a small specimen. It is one of the most beautiful flowering succulents, but not one of the easiest to grow, mainly because of the higher, draught-free winter temperature needed. However, given the right conditions, it will produce masses of red or pink blooms over a relatively long period during spring and summer. Plants can start to flower when only 15cm (6in) high. The thickened branching stems bear glossy bright green leaves; these normally fall during winter, when the potting mixture should be kept only slightly moist.

Grow in a good potting mixture, which can be either loam- or peat-based; to ensure the necessary free drainage it is worth mixing in about one third of sharp sand or perlite. Water can be given freely when the plant is in full growth and flower.

To encourage bloom:
Provide a winter rest. 11▸

Aechmea chantinii

(Amazonian zebra plant; Queen of the bromeliads)

- **Good light**
- **Temp: 13-18°C (55-65°F)**
- **Avoid overwatering**

Among the bromeliads this one has a reputation for being tough. It has very vicious spines along the leaf margins, which makes careful handling, and positioning, essential. The green-and-silver banded foliage itself makes a striking plant, but when the red-and-orange coloured bract appears one begins fully to appreciate the spectacle that this splendid plant displays.

Like all the more majestic plants in the bromeliad family, this will take several years to produce bracts following the purchase of a young plant. New plants can be started from offshoots that appear at the base of the parent stems of an older plant that has produced bracts. These should be planted individually in a loam-based potting mixture to which some prepared tree bark has been added. Pot as firmly as possible to prevent the plants toppling over, and keep out of direct sunlight until new growth is evident.

To encourage bloom:
Keep in bright light. 10▸

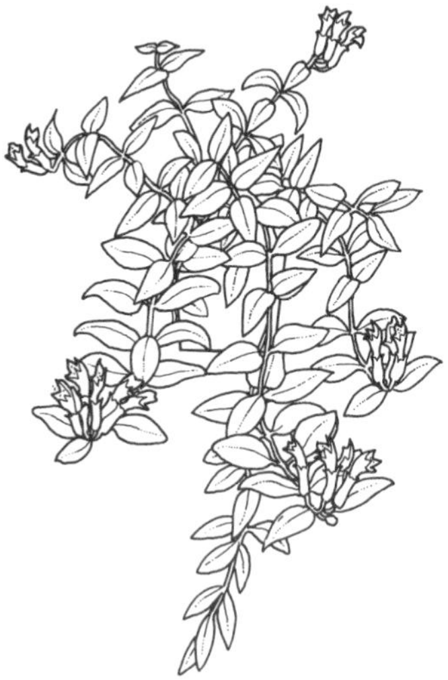

Aechmea fasciata

(Exotic brush; Silver vase; Urn plant; Vase plant)

- **Good light**
- **Temp: 13-18°C (55-65°F)**
- **Keep urn filled with water**

The silvery-grey leaves have a light grey down on them that adds much to the attraction of this most excellent of all bromeliads. Its grey leaves are broad and recurving and form a central chamber or urn, which should be filled with water. There are spines along the leaf margins, so be careful when handling. Also avoid touching the grey down on the leaves if the plants are to be seen to their best effect.

Young plants can be raised from seed, in which case bracts take some five to seven years to appear, or from basal shoots of mature plants, in which case bracts develop in two to three years.

The bract is a delightful soft pink in colour and, as if this were not enough, small but intensely blue flowers will also develop in the spiky pink bract. This is a truly fine plant that is easy to manage and will remain in 'flower' for up to nine months.

To encourage bloom:
Provide bright light and humid surroundings.

Aeschynanthus lobbianus

(Basket vine; Lipstick vine)

- **Light shade**
- **Temp: 16-21°C (60-70°F)**
- **Keep moist and fed**

These are temperamental plants that will produce exotic red flowers with seeming abandon one year, and in spite of having had identical treatment, will produce very little the next year. One of the supposed secrets of getting them to flower more reliably is to keep the plants very much on the dry side in winter and to lower the growing temperature. It is a procedure that works for many of the similar gesneriads, such as the columneas. During the warmer months, they should be kept out of bright sunlight.

The plants have glossy green leaves and have a natural pendulous habit, which adds considerably to their charm. New plants are easily started from cuttings a few centimetres in length that may be taken at any time during the spring or summer months. Arrange several cuttings to a small pot filled with peaty mixture and this will ensure that full and attractive plants develop.

To encourage bloom:
Give dry winter rest. 11▸

Allamanda cathartica

(Common allamanda; Golden trumpet)

- **Good light**
- **Temp: 16-21°C (60-70°F)**
- **Keep moist and fed**

The allamanda is better suited to the conservatory or sunroom than indoors. Using a loam-based potting compost this rapid grower will require ample moisture at its roots and frequent feeding while in active growth in spring and summer.

For best effect, train the active growth as it develops to a framework of some kind so that when the golden-yellow trumpet flowers appear they are set off to maximum effect. Although the flowers are sometimes sparse, there will generally be more of them if the plants are fed with a fertilizer recommended for flowering plants – something with a fairly high potash content, rather than nitrogen.

In winter, the amount of water given can be reduced and the plants can be severely pruned back to create a better shape and more manageable size.

To encourage bloom:
Keep in sunny conditions and repot each year into the next pot size.

Alpinia purpurata

(Red ginger)

- **Full sun**
- **Temp: 18-24°C (65-75°F)**
- **Water with care**

This ornamental plant from the ginger family, Zingiberaceae, provides a beautiful display of bright red bracts against a foil of glossy green leaves during the summer months. The real flowers are white and insignificant. Reaching a height of about 1.5m (5ft), this is a truly exotic subject.

To succeed, *Alpinia purpurata* needs plenty of sunshine; perhaps a sunroom or conservatory would be the ideal place in which to try this tropical plant. Use a large pot and an open potting mix of equal parts soil and humus. It is essential that this drains readily, for during the summer the plant should be watered freely but never allowed to remain waterlogged. During the winter rest it slightly, with less moisture.

Keep the temperature high, with a minimum of 18°C (65°F), and feed 'little and often' throughout the summer months. Propagate by dividing the rhizomes and replanting.

To encourage bloom:
Provide plenty of sunshine and warmth in the summer. 13▸

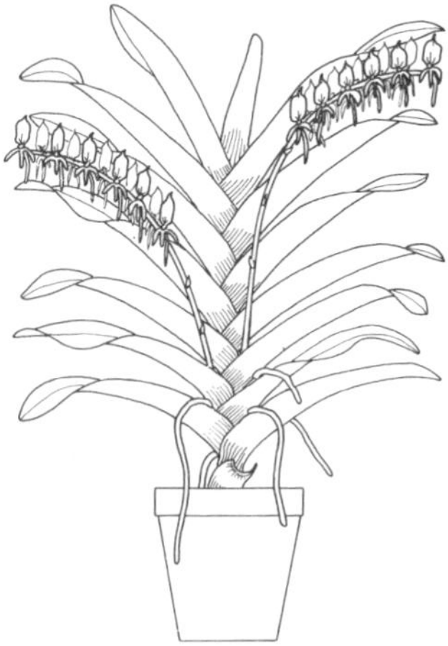

Angraecum eburneum

(Comet orchid)

- **Good light**
- **Temp: 18°C (65°F) min.**
- **Evergreen/no rest**

There are over 200 species of angraecums, although very few are seen in cultivation. They come mainly from tropical Africa.

This winter-flowering species resembles *Angraecum sesquipedale* in plant habit but the flower spikes are often longer, producing nine to 12 flowers about 10cm (4in) in diameter. The sepals, petals and spur are green and the lip pure white. Curiously, the flowers appear on the stem as if upside-down.

The plant thrives in generous conditions and should be watered throughout the year. During the summer months regular overhead spraying of the foliage and aerial roots is beneficial. The plant can also be foliar fed in the same way for nine months of the year. Although it likes a position in good light, the leaves are all too easily burnt if it is allowed to stand in bright sunlight for any length of time.

To encourage bloom:
Keep warm and humid. 13▶

Anguloa clowesii

(Cradle orchid; Tulip orchid)

- **Good light**
- **Temp: 11°C (52°F) min.**
- **Deciduous/rest in winter**

This is a small genus of about ten species, which grow naturally as epiphytes and terrestrials. They are high altitude plants from South America.

This large and beautiful species is commonly known as the 'cradle orchid' owing to the ability of the lip, which is loosely hinged, to rock back and forth when tilted. The lip is fully enclosed by the rest of the flower, which gives rise to a further popular name of 'tulip orchid'. The plant will grow well with lycastes but is considerably larger when in leaf.

Plenty of water and feed should be given during the growing season, when the plant is making up its large pseudobulbs. Water should be withheld when the leaves are shed at the end of the growing season. The flowers, 7.5cm (3in) across, appear singly from a stout stem at the same time as the new growth. They are a lovely canary yellow with a strong fragrance.

To encourage bloom:
Observe winter rest. 12▶

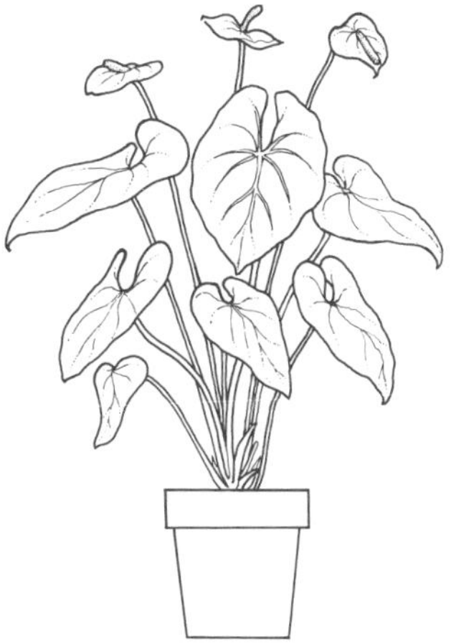

Anthurium andreanum

(Flamingo flower; Flamingo lily; Oilcloth flower; Painter's palette)

- **Light shade**
- **Temp: 18-24°C (65-75°F)**
- **Keep moist and fed**

One of the most spectacular of all the flowering plants grown in pots, this needs a temperature in excess of 18°C (65°F) and a high degree of humidity to give of its best. Flowers may be pink, white or red, with the latter being the colour most frequently seen.

As cut flowers *A. andreanum* has no peers. Flowers are borne on long stalks and from the time they are cut they have a full six weeks of life when placed in water, and will last much longer if left on the plant. Obtaining plants may be difficult, but they can be raised from seed and germinated in a temperature of not less than 24°C (75°F). However, it will be several years before the plants produce their exotic flowers. Leaves are large, carried on long petioles, and have an arrow-shaped appearance. Use an open leafy mix when potting on, and keep the plants well watered, misted, and away from direct sunlight.

To encourage bloom:
Provide humid conditions. 15▸

Anthurium scherzerianum

(Flamingo flower; Pigtail plant; Tailflower)

- **Light shade**
- **Temp: 16-21°C (60-70°F)**
- **Keep moist and fed**

This is the baby brother of *A. andreanum,* but is much better suited to average room conditions, in both space requirements and care. Green leaves are produced on short petioles from soil level, and flowers are generally red in colour and produced over a long spring and summer period. The spadix in the centre of the flower has a natural whorl to it that gives rise to one of its common names, 'pigtail plant'.

All anthuriums require an open potting mixture, and one made up of equal parts of peat and well-rotted leaves will be better than an entirely peat mix, or a mix containing loam. Once established, plants need regular feeding to maintain leaf colouring and to encourage production of flowers with stouter stems – weak-stemmed flowers will require support. Like *A. andreanum* this should be kept out of direct sunlight.

To encourage bloom:
Provide humid conditions.

Aphelandra squarrosa 'Louisae'

(Saffron spike; Zebra plant)

- **Light shade**
- **Temp: 16-21°C (60-70°F)**
- **Keep moist and fed**

The aphelandra has two fairly obvious common names, 'zebra plant' and 'saffron spike', relating to different parts of the plant – one to the grey-green leaves striped with silver, and the other to the saffron-yellow spike that forms the bract produced in midsummer. It is equally attractive with or without flowers, and reaches a height of about 60cm (2ft) when grown in a 13cm (5in) diameter pot. Larger pots will produce taller plants, usually in their second year.

When in good health all aphelandras will produce a wealth of roots and, consequently, require frequent feeding and potting on as soon as they have filled their existing pots with roots. Peaty mixtures are not much use to this plant; try a proprietary brand potting soil that contains a good proportion of loam. In spring and summer established plants must be fed with every watering.

To encourage bloom:
Rest after flowering. 14▶

Ardisia crispa/ crenata

(Coralberry; Spear flower)

- **Light shade**
- **Temp: 16-21°C (60-70°F)**
- **Keep moist and fed**

Although flowers are produced, the main attractions of this plant are the glossy green crenellated leaves and the long-lasting berries. It grows very slowly, and plants take several years to attain the maximum height of around 90cm (3ft). A stiff, upright central stem carries the woody branches, which will always be neat.

Offer a lightly shaded location for best results, and at no time be tempted to water excessively. Slow-growing plants of this kind are best kept on the dry side, particularly in winter. It is also important not to be too heavy-handed when feeding, and it should be discontinued altogether in winter. Plants with a slow growth rate are better grown in pots that are on the small side, and soil with a good percentage of loam must be used, as plants will quickly deteriorate in peat mixtures. Cuttings of firm young shoots can be taken in spring and rooted in peat at a temperature of not less than 21°C (70°F) to produce new plants.

To encourage bloom:
Use a small pot. 14▶

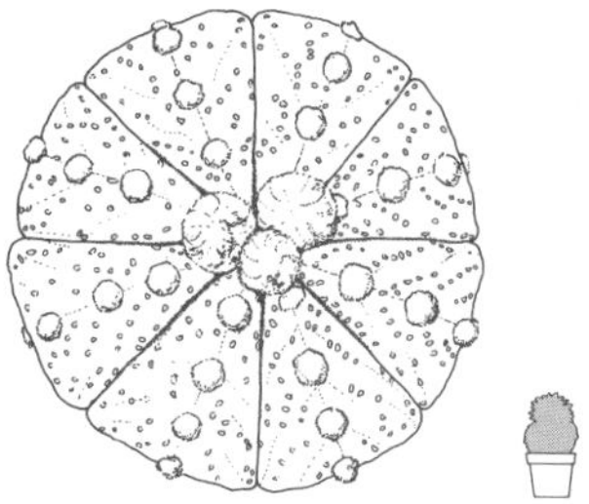

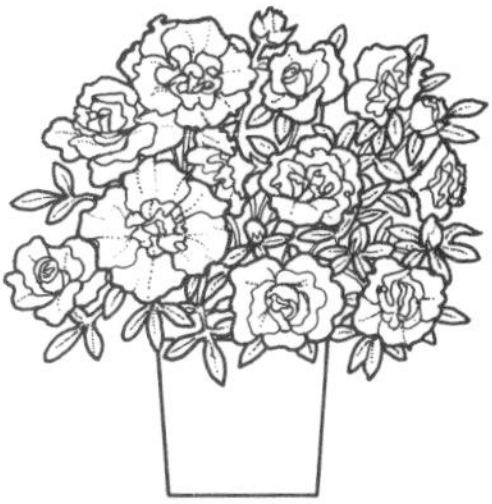

Astrophytum asterias

(Sand dollar cactus; Sea urchin cactus)

- **Full sun**
- **Temp: 5-30°C (41-86°F)**
- **Do not overwater**

Astrophytum asterias looks like a grey-green sea urchin; it could never be confused with any other cactus. Eventually it forms a flattened hemisphere about 10cm (4in) across. The stem is made up of eight spineless ribs, and the skin is covered with white spots. These vary from plant to plant: some specimens are beautifully covered in white polka dots, whereas others may have very few markings. The flowers open continuously through the summer; they are pale shiny yellow with a red throat, and sweetly scented. Seedlings about 2.5cm (1in) across will flower.

Never overwater and keep the soil completely dry during winter. A very open soil, half loam- or peat-based mixture and half sharp sand or perlite, is suitable. To ensure continuous flowering, keep the plant in the sunniest part of the greenhouse and feed every two weeks with a tomato fertilizer when the buds form.

To encourage bloom:
Provide plenty of sun.

Azalea indica

(Rhododendron simsii)

(Indian azalea)

- **Good light**
- **Temp: 10-16°C (50-60°F)**
- **Keep very moist**

For a colourful display there is little that can match these plants when they are well grown. With its evergreen foliage and flowers in many colours, the azalea will be more attractive and last very much longer if given cool and light conditions indoors – hot conditions definitely shorten the life of the flowers. The most sensible way of watering is to grasp the pot in both hands and plunge it in a bucket of water and leave it submerged until every vestige of air has escaped from the soil. Depending on conditions, it may be necessary to repeat this exercise two or three times weekly during the spring and summer months, with only slightly less water being given in winter.

Remove dead flowers as they occur and place plants out in the garden for the summer, being sure to bring them in before frosts occur. Use a mix of peat and well-rotted leaves when potting on.

To encourage bloom:
Keep cool and light. 16▸

Begonia boweri

(Eyelash begonia)

- **Filtered light**
- **Temp: 13-18°C (55-65°F)**
- **Keep moist**

There are a number of evergreen, fibrous-rooted begonias worth finding space for in the home, and this is one of the best of the more compact types. Flowers are white to pale pink in colour and though small in size, plentiful in number. The principal attraction, however, is the foliage, which is a mottled pale green and almost black in colour.

Growth is low and spreading, and the rhizomatous stem becomes gnarled in time, which tends to make plants less attractive as they shed their lower leaves. Rather than continue with an older and less attractive plant it is better to start fresh plants from sections of stem with a few leaves attached, or from individual leaves. Place leaves in shallow pans of fresh, moist peat at a temperature of not less than 18°C (65°F), and preferably in a closed propagator. Use peaty soil when potting on, and the plants will need moderate feeding and watering.

To encourage bloom:
Allow to grow potbound. 16▶

Begonia 'Fireglow'

- **Good light**
- **Temp: 13-18°C (55-65°F)**
- **Keep moist and fed**

Developed on the European Continent, this plant has provided something of a revolution with the improvement of growing techniques and the appearance of more varied flower colouring on the scene. In the original version, there were only single red flowers but now there are single and double flowers in a wide variety of attractive shades.

In good light plants flower for many months through spring and summer, but a constant guard must be kept against mildew, which manifests itself as a white powdery patch on leaves – treat with a suitable fungicide. To combat mildew further, offer light and fresh air as opposed to stuffy and hot conditions. Dead flowers resting on lower leaves will also cause rotting of foliage.

Use peaty soil when potting and keep moist and feed moderately. Cut back in autumn after flowering and keep on the dry side over winter.

To encourage bloom:
Grow in bright light.

Begonia coccinea 'Orange Rubra'

(Angelwing begonia)

- **Filtered light**
- **Temp: 16-21°C (60-70°F)**
- **Keep moist and fed**

With glossy green leaves and lovely orange-coloured flowers this is one of the taller growing fibrous-rooted begonias (sometimes referred to as cane-type begonias). *Begonia* 'Orange Rubra' is only one example of the many cane-type begonias to be seen in florists' and nurseries, and will offer a splendid show when in flower.

As the plants age they will have a natural tendency to shed their lower leaves, which will result in less attractive, bare stems, and this is one very good reason for raising fresh plants from easily rooted cuttings at regular intervals. Cuttings with three or four firm leaves can be taken at almost any time if a heated propagating case is available. Use rooting powder on the severed end of the cutting before inserting it in peat with a little sand added. When potting cuttings on it is advisable to put several cuttings in a pot for a fuller and more attractive display.

To encourage bloom:
Keep in a humid but not stuffy atmosphere. 33▸

Begonia semperflorens

(Wax begonia)

- **Good light**
- **Temp: 10-16°C (50-60°F)**
- **Keep moist and fed**

Often much in evidence as a summer bedding plant, this species is also excellent for decorating windowsills indoors when grown in a pot. In fact, an interesting use for *B. semperflorens* is to grow them out of doors as bedding plants during the summer months and to dig a few up and pot them before frosts occur. The foliage can be severely cut back, and in a surprisingly short time fresh growth will develop and eventually fresh flowers will appear and last for several weeks.

Many have bronze-coloured foliage that greatly enhances the plants. All must have ample light, especially during the darker months of the year. The temperature can be quite low, providing the soil is not allowed to become excessively wet. Remember to give a weak liquid feed at every watering. For new plants, sow seed in the spring.

To encourage boom:
Give plenty of light. 33▸

Beloperone guttata

(Shrimp plant)
- **Light shade**
- **Temp: 16-21°C (60-70°F)**
- **Keep moist and fed**

The common name of 'shrimp plant' derives from the shrimp-like bracts that are freely produced on vigorous plants. On the more common 'shrimp plant' bracts are a dullish red in colour, but there is also *B. g. lutea,* which has interesting greenish yellow bracts.

Purchased plants should have their roots inspected immediately, and if a mass of roots is in evidence the plants must be potted without delay into a loam-based mixture. Failure to do so will mean leaf discolouration and a general decline of the plant. Regular feeding is also of the utmost importance, and avoid dank, airless conditions. Growing tips of young plants should be removed to encourage a more bushy appearance. And if one has the courage to do so it will strengthen young plants if all the early bracts that develop are removed.

To encourage bloom:
Prune rigorously each year for compact, free-flowering plants.

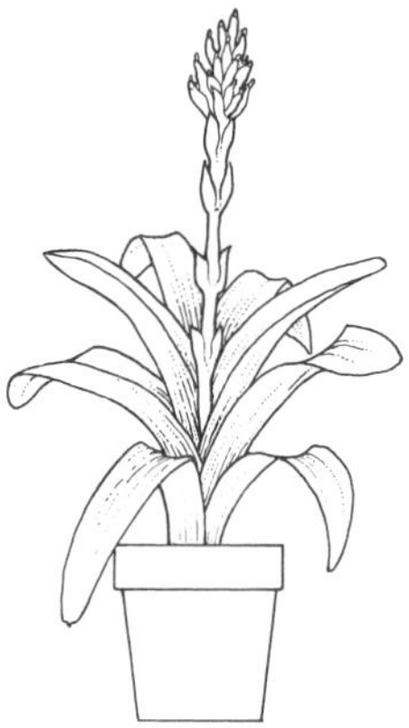

Billbergia pyramidalis

- **Good light**
- **Temp: 13-18°C (55-65°F)**
- **Keep on the dry side**

Belonging to the bromeliad family, billbergias are very tolerant houseplants that will thrive more on neglect than on constant, fussing care. This species has golden green leaves and produces attractive spikes of orange-pink bracts and red and blue flowers at almost any time of the year. Individual bracts last for only a week or so, but each mature plant bears several spikes.

Grow this bromeliad in loose-textured, lime-free potting mix and water only when the top layer of soil has dried out. Use soft water or rain water if possible. Normal room temperatures and bright light will keep this plant perfectly healthy.

Billbergias are generally free of pests and diseases. Propagation is also no problem; simply remove and pot up the offsets that develop around the base of the parent plant.

To encourage bloom:
Keep in bright light. 34▸

Bougainvillea

(Paper flower)

- **Sunny location**
- **Temp: 13-18°C (55-65°F)**
- **Keep dry in winter**

Few flowering plants are capable of giving a display that equals that of the paper-thin bracts of the bougainvillea, particularly when seen in its natural tropical habitat.

In pots they can be more difficult to manage if the owner is someone who is forever watering. These plants should be well watered and allowed to dry reasonably before repeating, and when the foliage turns colour and drops in the autumn it is a sign that water should be withheld until the following early spring when new growth appears and watering can begin again. Pruning – it tolerates quite severe cutting back – can be done in the autumn. Repotting can be undertaken in spring, and is best done by removing some of the old soil and potting the plant into the same container with a fresh loam-based mixture. During the summer months fresh air and full sunlight are essential.

To encourage bloom:
Provide several hours sunshine a day during summer. 35▸

Bouvardia domestica

(Jasmine plant; Trompetilla)

- **Light shade**
- **Temp: 13-18°C (55-65°F)**
- **Keep moist and fed**

These compact, shrubby plants produce flowers of many colours on the end of slightly drooping stems. They are ideal for a window location that offers good light and a modicum of fresh air, but not necessarily cold conditions. An added bonus with the bouvardia is that it is autumn flowering, so providing a display when there are fewer flowering pot plants around.

During the summer months established plants will be better for being placed out of doors in a sheltered position – in colder areas they will need the protection of an unheated greenhouse.

Plants should be watered freely and fed regularly during the summer months, less water and no feeding being required during winter. Plants are best potted in the spring, and a loam-based mixture will suit them better than an all-peat preparation. Spring is also the time to take cuttings or divide the roots.

To encourage bloom:
Pinch out growing tips in summer for autumn bloom.

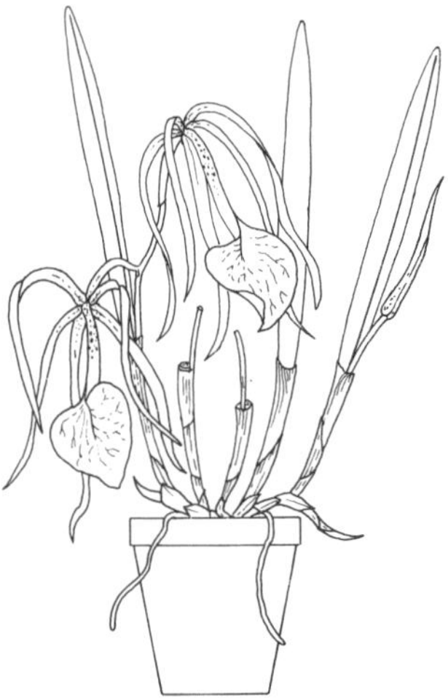

Brassavola nodosa

(Lady of the night)

- **Good light**
- **Temp: 13°C (55°F) min.**
- **Evergreen/dry rest**

Brassavolas are very popular with amateur growers, partly because they are easy to cultivate and also for the strange shapes of some of the flowers. The 15 species known are either epiphytic or lithophytic and come from Central and South America.

In this species the pseudobulbs and leaves are very slender and appear as one, both being cylindrical in shape. The plants are best grown on tree-fern fibre, with just a little compost, and suspended from the greenhouse roof. Brassavolas object to excessive moisture and should be kept quite dry during their lengthy period of rest.

Brassavola nodosa is very fragrant, especially in the cool of the evening or at night. It can be found in flower at any time of the year. The flowers, often four to five on a stem, are creamy-green and up to 7.5cm (3in) across when fully open. The lip is white with purple spots.

To encourage bloom:
Observe rest period. 34▸

Browallia speciosa

(Bush violet)

- **Good light**
- **Temp: 13-18°C (55-65°F)**
- **Keep moist and fed**

The flower colouring of *B. speciosa* ranges from blue to violet-blue, but there are white varieties available. It should be reasonably easy to raise new plants from seed on the windowsill for the person who is moderately competent with indoor plants. Sow seed in spring in peat to which a little sharp sand has been added, and after sowing just cover the seed with a fine layer of sand. Place a sheet of glass over the container holding the seed, and over the glass place a sheet of newspaper until the seed has germinated. When large enough to handle, the seedlings can be pricked off into a very peaty mixture with reasonable space for seedlings to develop. Subsequently, transfer the tiny plants to small pots filled with loam-based mixture and allow to grow on.

From then on keep them moist, fed, and in good light. Discard the plants after they have flowered.

To encourage bloom:
Keep plants cool and fed during the summer months. 36▸

Calanthe vestita

- **Good light**
- **Temp: 18°C (65°F) min.**
- **Deciduous/dry rest**

With tall, upright flower spikes and many long-lasting flowers, *Calanthe* is deservedly a special favourite with orchid growers. Given warm-house conditions, it grows easily and is thus a good plant for beginners. Of the 150 species known, most are terrestrials; they come from a wide area, including South Africa, Asia and Central America.

The flowers of *Calanthe vestita* range in colour from white to deep pink, the lip often being stronger in colour than the rest of the flower.

A warm greenhouse with good light suits this plant best. This deciduous species produces rather large, angular pseudobulbs with wide, ribbed leaves. During the growing season the plant should be liberally watered and fed until the leaves turn yellow and fall during the early winter months. At this stage watering should be gradually reduced. After flowering the pseudobulbs should be repotted in a well-drained compost.

To encourage bloom:
Observe rest period. 36▸

Calceolaria hybrids

(Pocketbook plant; Pouch flower; Slipper flower; Slipperwort)

- **Good light**
- **Temp: 10-16°C (50-60°F)**
- **Keep moist and fed**

These pouch-like flowers are available in a bewildering range of colours. Many different strains are available and all will give a splendid display if a few standard rules are followed. First and foremost is that these plants must have good light, a loam-based mixture in which to grow, and regular feeding once they have filled their pots with roots.

When buying a mature plant from a retailer it is important to check the roots in the pot on getting the plant home; an overcrowded root system means the plant should be potted on straight away. It is also wise to give plants a general inspection before buying, particularly on the undersides of leaves, and to reject any that have pests present.

These are temporary plants and should be discarded after flowering.

To encourage bloom:
Keep the plants cool and in bright light (but not direct sunlight). Water regularly to keep the soil moist.

Callistemon citrinus

(Bottlebrush; Crimson bottlebrush)

- **Good light**
- **Temp: 13-16°C (55-60°F)**
- **Keep moist and fed**

An Australian plant, the callistemon gets its common name of 'bottlebrush plant' from the formation of the unusual flower, which is in the shape of the brush used for cleaning out bottles.

It is a green-leaved woody shrub that will, in time, reach a height of about 150cm (5ft) if growing conditions are agreeable. Position it in a light, although not necessarily sunny, location, and it will be better if the growing temperature is around 16°C (60°F), as warmer temperatures tend to produce softer and less attractive plants.

The soil should be kept moist, but not saturated for long periods, though much will depend on the growing position; in sunnier spots it will obviously be necessary to water more often. Use free-draining loam-based mixture when potting on. When established, the plants need frequent feeding.

To encourage bloom:
Keep the plant fairly cool in airy surroundings. 37▸

Camellia japonica

(Common camellia; Tea plant)

- **Good light**
- **Temp: 10-16°C (50-60°F)**
- **Keep moist with rain water**

These make fine garden plants in sheltered areas if the soil in which they are growing is acid rather than alkaline.

Perhaps not so good for the indoor location, they are nevertheless excellent plants for porches and conservatories that offer a little shelter from the elements. Plants that are grown from seed sown in the spring, or from cuttings rooted in the autumn, can be purchased in small pots from good retailers.

With careful handling these small plants can be gradually potted on until they are in containers of 25cm (10in) in diameter – use the acid soil recommended for camellias at each potting stage, and collect rain water for watering.

In time plants of about 150cm (5ft) in height will have developed, and in early spring there can surely be nothing more appealing than camellia blooms in white, pink or red.

To encourage bloom:
Maintain cool conditions. 37▸

Right: **Begonia semperflorens**
Long an outdoor favourite, the wax begonia is small and pretty. The flowers appear on and off for many months making it a valuable asset in the indoor garden. 27▸

Below: **Begonia 'Orange Rubra'**
A fine angelwing begonia with handsome leaves spotted in white, and cascades of orange flowers. 27▸

Above: **Brassavola nodosa**
Small but with charm, this orchid has needlelike leaves and heavenly scented white flowers that perfume the whole room at night. 30▸

Left: **Billbergia pyramidalis**
Golden-green leaves and orange-pink flower bracts make this easy to grow bromeliad a favourite. 28▸

Right: **Bougainvillea**
This popular red or purple flowering climbing plant is perfect for the sunny window. With careful culture it will bloom freely throughout the summer. Needs support; very tropical and pretty. 29▸

Above: **Browallia speciosa**
This delightful plant is now available in compact hybrids that flower freely. They can be placed outdoors during the summer months. 30▸

Below: **Calanthe vestita**
Do not let the fact that this orchid is deciduous deter you; it makes up for its bareness in winter with dainty pink-purple and white blooms. 31▸

Above: **Callistemon citrinus**
Brilliant colour makes callistemon a popular plant, but it is large and requires space. Blooming in summer or autumn and rather unusual, it adds interest to the indoor garden. 32▸

Right: **Camellia japonica**
Many varieties of fine flowering evergreens for that cool location. Flower colours range from white to red. Outstanding. 32▸

Above: **Cattleya Bob Betts 'Mont Millais'**
Known as the corsage flower, cattleyas are always sure to please the indoor gardener. The flowers are large and generally fragrant. C. Bob Betts 'Mont Millais' is a fine white and a parent of many cattleya hybrids. 50▸

Left: **Capsicum annuum**
This lovely decorative plant has handsome brilliant red, yellow or purple fruit in winter. 49▸

Above: **Catharanthus roseus**
Rose red flowers in summer make this a fine seasonal plant for indoors. New plants are best started from cuttings or seed each year. Unusual and worth the space. 50▶

Above: **Celosia argentea 'Pyramidalis'**
The red or yellow flowers resemble plumes. An ideal plant for the windowsill, as dwarf varieties grow to only 30cm (12in). Generally pale green, the leaves of some varieties are a beautiful bronze. 51▸

Above: **Columnea microphylla**
With tiny leaves and bright scarlet and yellow flowers, this trailing gesneriad creates a sensation. Needs warm, humid conditions. 56▸

Below: **Citrus mitis**
A handsome small tree, C. mitis bears tiny oranges in winter, making it a decorative windowsill plant. Ideal for small places. Easy to grow. 53▸

Above: **Coelogyne ochracea**
Pretty as a picture, this dainty harbinger of spring has yellow and white flowers. A fine orchid. 55▸

Left: **Crocus**
Yellow crocuses are usually the earliest to bloom of the large-flowered varieties. Bring them into the warm only when the buds begin to show colour. 57▸

Right: **Clivia miniata**
If you can't grow anything, this plant will make you a gardener. Easy to bloom each spring with magnificent clusters of orange flowers. Handsome straplike dark green leaves. Highly recommended. 54▸

Above: **Cymbidium hybrids**
This large group of orchids offers handsome long-lasting flowers in an array of colours. The miniature hybrid shown here is called Elmwood, an easy to grow and very elegant variety. 59▸

Left: **Cuphea ignea**
The black and white ashlike tips of the red tubular flowers give this abundantly blooming plant its common name of cigar flower. 58▸

Right: **Cyclamen persicum**
Cyclamen grow wild in Greece and along the eastern shores of the Mediterranean. Hybrids from these are highly prized indoor flowering plants. They come in beautiful pastel shades; always desirable. 58▸

Above: **Echinocereus baileyi**
A lovely 20cm (8in) cylindrical cactus with violet-pink flowers. 61▸

Below: **Echeveria 'Doris Taylor'**
Perhaps the best known of the echeverias, with handsome spoon shaped foliage and red and yellow flowers in spring. 60▸

Above right:
Dendrobium Gatton Sunray
This colourful dendrobium is hard to resist. With a little extra care the plant will bloom twice a year. 59▸

Right: **Encyclia cochleata**
The cockleshell orchid is easy and superb for unusual flowers. 62▸

Above: **Episcia cupreata**
This is one of the popular episcias, with fine scarlet flowers and leaves that look sugar-coated. 63▸

Left: **Episcia dianthiflora**
From tropical Mexico, this white flowering episcia is a favourite houseplant; decorative foliage adds to its appeal. Use it in hanging containers for maximum display. 63▸

Campanula isophylla

(Bellflower; Falling stars; Italian bellflower; Star-of-Bethlehem; Trailing campanula)

- **Good light**
- **Temp: 10-16°C (50-60°F)**
- **Keep moist, but dry in winter**

This exquisite plant is available in both pale blue and white colouring. The species is quite tough, but will be happier in lower temperatures, around 10°C (50°F), than it will be if grown in hot, stuffy rooms.

The leaves are small and pale green in colour and flowers are bell-shaped and produced continuously over a very long period from spring through into autumn. To encourage the maximum number of flowers, it is advisable to remove all dead flowers as soon as they appear.

Set off to best effect when grown in hanging baskets or containers, these plants will need frequent watering and ample feeding during spring and summer.

In the autumn when they are becoming more miserable in appearance they can be severely cut back, kept on the dry side, then repotted in the spring to start life all over again.

To encourage bloom:
Pinch off flowers as they fade.

Capsicum annuum

(Ornamental chilli; Red pepper)

- **Good light**
- **Temp: 10-16°C (50-60°F)**
- **Keep moist and fed**

These bright red-fruited plants are raised from seed sown in the spring in temperatures of not less than 21°C (70°F). When large enough to handle, the tiny seedlings are transferred from their initial boxes or pans to small pots filled with loam-based mixture, and subsequently go on into 13-18cm (5-7in) pots depending on the size of the plants required.

When in their final pots, it is much better to place the plants out of doors in full sun for the summer months, plunging pots in peat to reduce the amount of watering needed.

At all times full light is essential, and this is of particular importance once the fruits have formed, as they fall alarmingly when light is poor – during fog for example. Discard these plants at the end of the growing season.

To encourage bloom:
Give ample sun and ventilation. 38▸

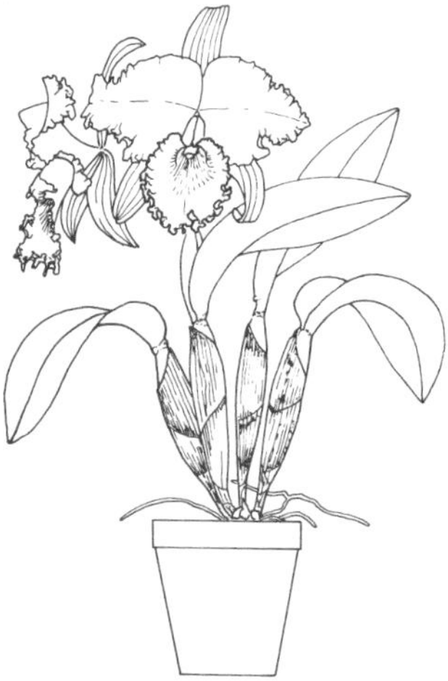

Catharanthus roseus

(Vinca rosea)

(Madagascar periwinkle)

- **Sunny location**
- **Temp: 13-18°C (55-65°F)**
- **Keep moist and fed**

This is a charming, trouble-free little plant that may be easily grown from seed sown in the spring or from tip cuttings taken at the same time of year. Cuttings of about 7.5cm (3in) in length should be taken from plants of the previous year and inserted in peat and sand mixture at a temperature of about 21°C (70°F).

Leaves are a bright glossy green and flowers may be either white or pink. It is really best to treat these as annuals so that fresh plants are raised in the spring each year and older plants discarded. A loam-based potting mixture will suit them best and once they have got under way it is advisable to remove the growing tips to encourage a more compact shape. They should be kept on a bright windowsill; while in active growth keep moist and feed with a weak liquid fertilizer at each watering.

To encourage bloom:
Raise new young plants. Feed well when growing actively. 39▸

Cattleya hybrids

(Corsage flower)

- **Good filtered light**
- **Temp: 13°C (55°F) min.**
- **Evergreen/some rest**

The cattleya hybrids produce spectacular flowers up to 15cm (6in) across, ranging in colour from deep lavenders and pinks through to pure glistening white.

For best results grow these plants in a greenhouse and provide stable temperature conditions, with 13°C (55°F) as a winter night minimum. Maintain a humid but buoyant atmosphere. Bright filtered light is preferable to direct sun. Using medium-grade fir bark as the potting mix, they can be grown in various containers such as pots, pans and baskets. Good drainage is essential.

By choosing a selection from the many hybrids available, it is possible to enjoy a display of these stunning flowers throughout the year. Many of the hybrids need a resting period after they have flowered. The plants are not usually bothered by insect pests.

To encourage bloom:
Keep plants dry while in flower. 38▸

Celosia argentea

(Cockscomb; Plume celosia; Prince of Wales' feathers)

- **Good light**
- **Temp: 10-16°C (50-60°F)**
- **Keep moist and fed**

The variety *C. argentea* 'Cristata' is generally referred to as the 'cockscomb' because the bract it produces resembles the comb of the cockerel. The variety 'Pyramidalis' has plumed flowers in red or yellow. In any event, these are annual plants that are produced in large quantities both for indoor decoration in pots and for use as a bedding plant in the garden.

Over the years there have been many new varieties of this plant, but most have a somewhat grotesque appearance and leave much to be desired, but they clearly have attraction for some indoor-plant growers. Cheapness has some bearing on *C. argentea*'s popularity. Although it is discarded after flowering, the plant is very easily raised from seed sown in the spring. Seedlings are subsequently pricked off, and grown on in larger pots – the eventual size of pot dictating to some extent the dimensions of the mature plant.

To encourage bloom:
Keep cool and bright. 40▸

Chamaecereus silvestrii

(Peanut cactus)

- **Full sun**
- **Temp: 0-30°C (32-86°F)**
- **Keep dry in winter**

Sometimes recently listed as *Lobivia silvestrii* (another victim of botanical name changes), it seems more appropriate here to use the name of so many years standing. The spreading stems are somewhat finger-like in shape and size, bright green in colour and covered with short spines. Offsets, somewhat resembling green peanuts, appear along the length of the stems, hence the popular name. They detach themselves at the slightest touch, and can be potted up at once – surely the easiest cactus to propagate! But the great joy of this plant is the brilliant scarlet flowers, 4cm (1.6in) across; produced in profusion, they almost cover the stems during spring and summer.

This is not a fussy plant, so grow it in any good potting mixture. Water freely in spring and summer. One of the hardiest cacti, it will survive in a cold frame if quite dry.

To encourage bloom:
Keep plants cold in winter to encourage good flowering.

Chrysanthemum

(Florist's mum)

- **Good light**
- **Temp: 13-18°C (55-65°F)**
- **Keep moist**

This has become one of the world's most popular flowering pot plants, mainly because it can be produced at any time of the year by commercial growers with the right sort of equipment and facilities.

The natural flowering time of this plant is from late summer through the autumn when about two thirds of the day is dark. It is these conditions that cause chrysanthemum flower buds to initiate and subsequently come into flower. However, by using black polythene to cover plants over and reduce the amount of daylight, the grower can simulate autumn light conditions and induce plants to flower at an unnatural time. Additional artificial lighting can be used to extend the day length if required.

Trouble-free indoors, these plants need good light, moisture, and weak feeding. Plant in the garden after flowering; they will survive where winter conditions allow but dwarfed forms will grow tall.

To encourage bloom:
Keep plants very moist.

Cineraria

(Senecio cruentus)

- **Good light**
- **Temp: 13-18°C (55-65°F)**
- **Keep moist and fed**

The compact, coarse green leaves and bright daisy flowers of this plant make it one of the most popular pot plants among the cheaper range. Ideally, seed should be sown in early spring and plantlets pricked off and potted on as they establish themselves.

Seed should be chosen wisely, and where growing space is limited the more miniature varieties should be selected. Seed of larger-growing types will develop into plants of splendid size in time if potted on and given regular feeding. A loam-based mixture is important as these are greedy plants that thrive on ample nourishment, both from the soil in which they are growing and from the subsequent feeding that they receive.

When raised in a greenhouse the cineraria can become the host for every pest that has ever been thought of, so inspect plants regularly and treat accordingly.

To encourage bloom:
Keep cool and fed.

Citrus mitis

(Citrofortunella mitis)

(Calamondin orange)

- **Sunny location**
- **Temp: 13-18°C (55-65°F)**
- **Keep moist and fed**

Citrus mitis is one of the most decorative of potted plants when its branches are festooned with perfectly shaped miniature oranges. The glossy green foliage will become yellow if underfed, particularly from magnesium deficiency – to combat this deficiency treat with sequestered iron.

Full light is essential, but foliage may become scorched if plants are placed too close to window panes on very sunny days. During the summer months plants will do better if placed out of doors in full sun. While in the garden it is important not to neglect feeding and watering. Failure to keep the soil moist will result in shrivelling of leaves.

White, heavily scented flowers appear in late summer. To help with pollination draw your hands through the flowers periodically. Flowers are followed by small green fruits that will in time develop into miniature oranges – dozens of them!

To encourage bloom and fruit:
Put plants outdoors in the summer and keep them moist. 41▶

Clerodendron thomsoniae

(Bleeding heart vine; Glory bower)

- **Good light**
- **Temp: 16-21°C (60-70°F)**
- **Keep moist and fed**

This is a useful plant for spacious surroundings, or for training against the wall of a heated greenhouse or conservatory. It is a natural climbing plant, the stems of which will entwine themselves around any sort of climbing framework that may be provided.

New plants are started from cuttings taken from any firm shoots that are not producing flowers – a temperature of about 21°C (70°F) is needed to encourage rooting. When a reasonable amount of root is evident the young plants can be potted into small pots filled with loam-based potting soil.

In the early stages of growth a temperature minimum of 18°C (65°F) should be the aim, with a slightly lower level for plants that are established in larger containers. The plant has coarse green leaves attached to woody stems, but the red and white flowers that develop in clusters are the main attraction. Prune to shape after flowering.

To encourage bloom:
Prune after blooming is over.

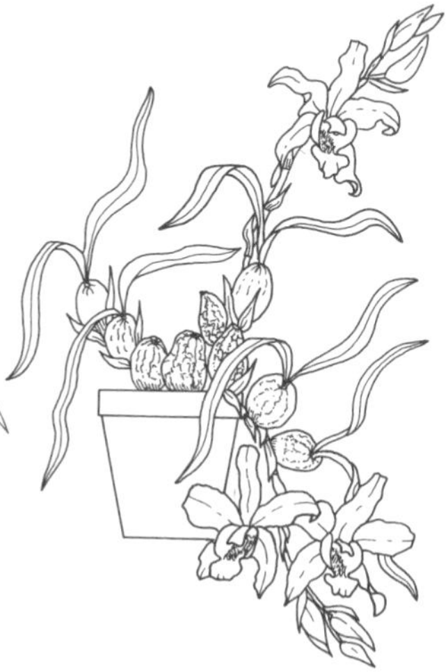

Clivia miniata

(Kaffir lily)

- **Shade**
- **Temp: 16-21°C (60-70°F)**
- **Keep moist**

To encourage these plants to flower freely, keep their roots in pot-bound condition – not a very difficult task as they very quickly make sufficient root to fill existing containers. Getting these plants to produce their exotic orange bell-flowers is always a problem, but older plants will usually reward the patience expended on them in the end.

Leaves are thick, broad, and strap-like and are produced from very large bulbous stems at soil level. Clean leaves with a damp cloth to keep them looking their best. Inevitably, plants will require quite large pots as they mature, and when potting on it is advisable to use a loam-based mixture that will sustain the plant over a longer period of time.

Having outgrown their pots and perhaps their allotted space indoors, the bulbous clumps can be divided to make new plants.

To encourage bloom:
Grow slightly potbound and keep dry during winter rest. 43▸

Coelogyne cristata

- **Good light**
- **Temp: 10°C (50°F) min.**
- **Evergreen/dry rest**

Perhaps the most familiar of the genus, this species likes to grow on undisturbed into a specimen plant. The flower spike appears from the centre of the new growth and its snowy-white flowers, broken only by a blotch of golden yellow at the centre of the lip, appear in mid-winter and last for four or five weeks.

Although the genus contains well over 100 species, few coelogynes are found in collections today. This is a pity, for they are orchids of great merit. They are, in the main, easy to grow and many species thrive in cool conditions, requiring a warmer environment only during their active growing season. Rest well in winter to achieve flowering.

Many coelogynes are suitable for growing on into specimen plants. However, be warned: a specimen plant of one of the larger-growing species can take up a considerable amount of space in the greenhouse. Fortunately, it is possible to choose from a wide range of smaller-growing species.

To encourage bloom:
Observe winter rest period.

Coelogyne ochracea

- **Good light**
- **Temp: 10°C (50°F) min.**
- **Evergreen/dry rest**

This popular species from India has shiny green pseudobulbs topped by a pair of leaves. The flower spikes are produced freely from the new growth while it is very young. Like all coelogynes, it prefers to be grown on into a specimen plant with as little disturbance as possible, although this species is unlikely to become unmanageable in size. The flowers are extremely pretty and full of fragrance.

After flowering grow the plant on well into the autumn, by which time the season's growth will have matured and the plant will rest. Place in full light for the winter and withhold all water until the new growths appear in early spring. The pseudobulbs will shrivel during this time but they will quickly plump up again when normal watering is resumed.

Ideal for beginners, it is equally at home growing indoors or in a cool greenhouse.

To encourage bloom:
Keep plant dry at the roots durings its winter rest period.

Columnea banksii

(Goldfish vine)

- **Light shade**
- **Temp: 16-21°C (60-70°F)**
- **Keep moist, but drier in winter**

This much-neglected plant has many fine qualities, not least the fact that it is not at all difficult to rear and is almost totally free of pests. Evergreen, oval-shaped leaves are a dull green in colour and are attached to woody stems. Initially, the stems are supple and will hang naturally over the container in which the plant is growing, but in time they become rigid.

Besides the distinct advantage of being a natural hanging plant, this columnea will also oblige with a wealth of reddish-orange flowers in early spring when flowering houseplants are not so plentiful.

However, getting plants to produce their flowers can be a problem, but one way is to keep the soil very much on the dry side during winter and at the same time lower the growing temperature by several degrees. New plants are easily started from cuttings.

To encourage bloom:
Observe winter rest period.

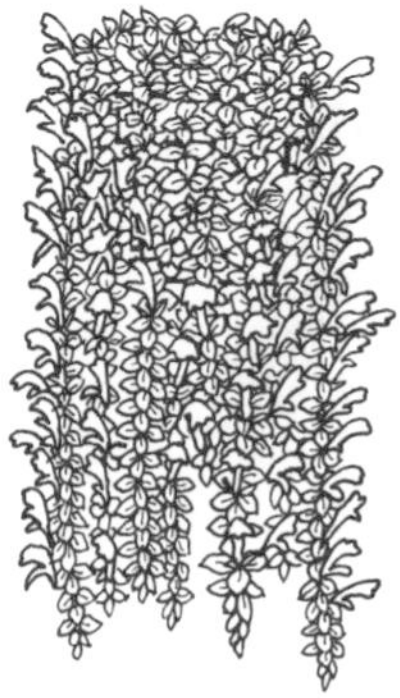

Columnea microphylla

(Goldfish vine)

- **Shade**
- **Temp: 18-21°C (65-70°F)**
- **Keep moist, drier in winter**

This is one of the more difficult columneas to grow successfully. The difficulty lies in the fact that it requires a constant temperature in the region of 18-21°C (65-70°F). Nevertheless, once the challenge is accepted, the results can be very rewarding. The small, oval-shaped, pale-green leaves are attached to wiry stems that hang perpendicularly from the container in which the plant is growing. Essentially, it is a hanging plant and can only be seen at its best when provided with a hanging pot or basket in which to grow.

Flowers, generally produced during the summer months, are rich orange and red in colour and on mature plants are produced in great abundance. Something that adds to their attraction is that mature plants in large baskets may have trails 1.8m (6ft) or more in length, and may well have flowers from top to bottom.

It is important to keep the soil moist and to feed regularly with weak liquid fertilizer.

To encourage bloom:
Keep dry during winter. 41▸

Crassula falcata

(Jade plant)

- **Full sun**
- **Temp: 7-30°C (45-86°F)**
- **Keep moist all year**

Crassula falcata has such colourful flowers that it is a popular 'florist's plant' and is the parent of many beautiful hybrids. It is a small shrub, 30cm (12in) high. The large bluish-grey leaves are sickle-shaped. The stout flower stem carries a mass of tiny scarlet flowers; each individual flower is bell-shaped and they are arranged in a large, flat inflorescence. If the plant is grown in a greenhouse border, it will branch.

The crassulas may be propagated from leaf or stem cuttings. Shrubby crassulas tend to become untidy with age and should be restarted in the early summer. Grow in a well-drained soil, two parts loam-based mixture to one part sharp sand or perlite. Keep moist all the year but allow to dry out between waterings and keep a little drier immediately after flowering. When the buds begin to form, feed with a liquid tomato fertilizer once every two weeks.

To encourage bloom:
Keep in a sunny window.

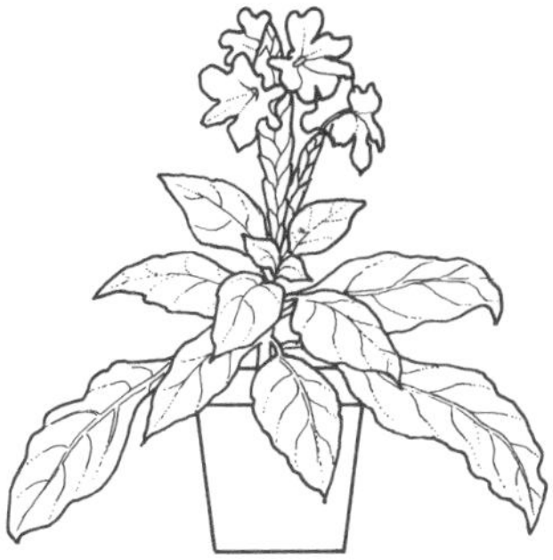

Crocus

- **Good light with sunshine**
- **Temp: 7-16°C (45-60°F)**
- **Keep moist while growing**

Flowering crocuses on the windowsill give a clear indication that spring is on the way, but one has to think of them in early autumn, when the corms are planted. Bold groups in shallow pans filled with houseplant soil are better than small pots with a few wispy leaves and flowers. They must be planted in early autumn and put in a dark, cool place outdoors to develop the essential roots before shoot growth begins.

A simple way of creating dark conditions is to place a black flower-pot over the pot holding the corms. Once growth begins, the corms can be exposed to the light and taken indoors, where they will quite quickly start to bloom. Flowers will last for a longer period in cool and airy conditions than in warmer, stuffy rooms. After flowering, the corms should be planted out in the garden, or stored to flower in new soil the following season.

To encourage bloom:
Keep corms dark and cool in early stages; then provide warmth and light as growth begins. 42▸

Crossandra infundibuliformis

(Firecracker flower)

- **Good light**
- **Temp: 16-21°C (60-70°F)**
- **Keep moist**

These are neat plants for the windowsill, needing light and airy conditions, with some protection from strong sunlight. The soil needs to be kept moist at all times, with less water being required in winter. In winter there will also be no need to feed plants, but while in active growth they will respond to feeding with weak liquid fertilizer. Vigorous plants will tolerate and benefit from feeding at every watering. An alternative to liquid feeding would be the use of tablet or stick-form fertilizers that are pressed into the soil and made available to the plant over a period of several weeks.

Naturally glossy green leaves are topped by bright orange flowers in the spring, with the possibility of further flowers later in the year. New plants can be started from seed or cuttings.

To encourage bloom:
Provide plants with good air circulation at all times.

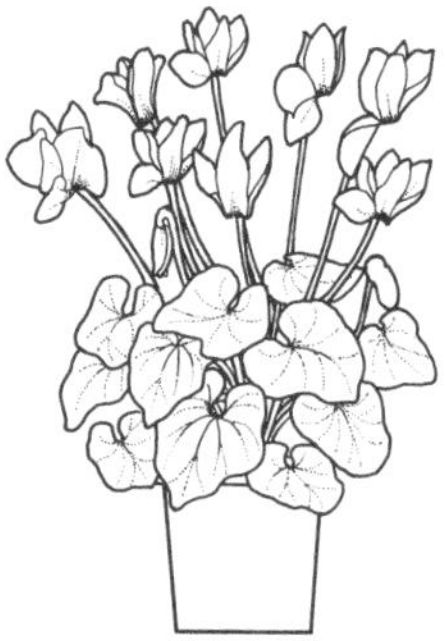

Cuphea ignea

(Cigar flower; Firecracker flower; Mexican cigar plant)

- **Good light**
- **Temp: 10-16°C (50-60°F)**
- **Keep moist and fed**

This is a straggly plant with a mass of tiny leaves pin-pointed with an abundance of red tubular flowers. The ends of the tubular flowers are lipped with blackish-grey colouring not unlike cigar ash – hence the appropriate common name of 'cigar flower'.

New plants can be raised from seed sown in the spring or from stem cuttings taken in late summer. When only one or two plants are required it is usually better to purchase established plants, so saving the bother of overwintering or raising seed plants.

Cupheas are very easy to manage on a light windowsill, needing no particular attention other than the usual watering and feeding. Once established in 13cm (5in) pots no further potting is needed, as plants will tend to become too large. Discard after flowering.

To encourage bloom:
Provide bright light. 44▸

Cyclamen persicum

(Alpine violet; Poor man's orchid; Shooting star)

- **Good light**
- **Temp: 10-16°C (50-60°F)**
- **Keep moist, but dry after flowering**

Ever popular, the cyclamen has a cool beauty that is matched by few other plants. Centrally heated rooms kept at excessively high temperature can be its worst enemy. On a cool windowsill that offers good light the life of the cyclamen indoors will be much extended.

Water well by pouring water on to the soil surface and ensuring that surplus water is seen to drain through the holes in the bottom of the pot; repeat only when the foliage feels limp to the touch. But never allow leaves and flowers to flag excessively.

Clear out dead flowers and leaves complete with their stems to prevent rotting. Following flowering, plants die back naturally and should be stored cool and dry until new growth is evident – which is also the time to pot on.

To encourage bloom:
Give plenty of water. Keep the plants cool and humid (but do not spray the flowers). Give resting period. 45▸

Cymbidium hybrids

- **Protect from strong sun**
- **Temp: 10°C (50°F) min.**
- **Evergreen/no rest**

Cymbidium hybrids have rightly gained a reputation throughout the world. There are hundreds to choose from, both large plants and the delightful, easy-care miniatures.

The miniature hybrid cymbidiums provide an alternative for the grower with limited space. Being smaller and more easily managed plants, they can be accommodated in the home. Their more compact blooms are just as rewarding, and are often of rich colouring.

To achieve regular flowering all cymbidiums should be repotted every other year. Use a potting mix of peat moss, sand, perlite and fir bark.

Cymbidiums, particularly if grown in the drier indoor atmosphere, can be prone to attacks from red spider mite. Regular sponging and wiping of the leaves with water, particularly the undersides, will keep this at bay.

To encourage bloom:
Give full light in winter, but provide shade in summer. 44▶

Dendrobium Gatton Sunray

- **Good light**
- **Temp: 13°C (55°F) min.**
- **Evergreen/dry winter rest**

A magnificent hybrid, this is the largest of the cultivated dendrobiums, and requires plenty of growing space. It is an extremely robust plant, the canes growing to a height of 2m (6.5ft) or more. The extremely large and showy flowers, which appear in trusses during the early summer, are more than 10cm (4in) across and last in perfection for about ten days. A large plant will produce numerous trusses, each carrying several flowers. This will extend the flowering period, as not all the trusses come into flower at the same time.

The plant succeeds best in an intermediate greenhouse where it can be given good light and a decided rest during the winter months. In view of its large size, this plant should not be attempted where adequate space and light cannot be given.

To encourage bloom:
Provide good light. 47▶

Dipladenia splendens 'Rosea'

(Pink allamande)

- **Good light**
- **Temp: 16-21°C (60-70°F)**
- **Keep moist and fed**

This is a natural climbing plant best suited to the heated conservatory or greenhouse, but a challenging plant that will be good for the ego of the houseplant-grower who cultivates it successfully. Indoors, it is best to confine the roots to pots of modest size so that growth is restricted. However, very small pots are often difficult to manage, so pots of 13cm (5in) diameter will be best.

For potting, use a loam-based mixture as opposed to a very peaty mix, which will tend to produce soft growth.

During the summer months healthy plants are festooned with attractive soft pink flowers, and these are the principal feature of the dipladenia. After flowering the plant can be pruned to shape, if needed.

The soil should be kept moist without being totally saturated for long periods, and regular feeding will be beneficial when growth is active.

To encourage bloom:
Keep in a sunny place.

Echeveria 'Doris Taylor'

- **Full sun**
- **Temp: 5-30°C (41-86°F)**
- **Never allow to dry out**

Echeverias are such charming small pot plants that a number of hybrids have been developed. 'Doris Taylor' is a cross between *E. setosa* and *E. pulvinata*. It is a freely branching plant that looks its best in a half-pot. The pale green leaves are densely covered with white hairs and are carried on reddish-brown stems to form neat rosettes. The reddish-orange flowers are bell-shaped, and open in the spring.

'Doris Taylor' should be grown in loam-based potting mixture in a light position – either in a greenhouse or on a windowsill. Water generously during spring and summer, and feed every two weeks with a high-potassium fertilizer. Keep slightly moist in winter. During the winter, the lower leaves shrivel: they should be removed or fungus will grow on them, which can cause the death of the plant. In spring, the plant will be leggy. Behead the main rosette and remove the smaller ones for potting.

To encourage bloom:
Give plenty of sun. 46▸

Echinocereus baileyi

(Rainbow cactus)
- **Full sun**
- **Temp: 5-30°C (41-86°F)**
- **Keep dry in winter**

This small desert cactus grows to a height of about 20cm (8in) and produces satiny, sharp-pink flowers during the summer.

Good drainage is essential, so grow it in a mixture of two parts good quality potting material (peat or loam-based) and one part sharp sand or perlite. Cover the surface of the mix with a layer of gravel to protect the base of the plant against stem rot. Keep the plant in a sunny window and water during the summer, but only when the soil is dry. When buds form, feed every two weeks with a high-potassium fertilizer.

Rest the plant during the winter, giving little or no water in a cooler location. Propagate by detaching offsets and potting up separately. This plant is generally pest and disease-free.

To encourage bloom:
Provide full sun and feed when buds start to appear. 46▸

Echinopsis hybrids

(Sea urchin cactus; Thistle globe)
- **Full sun**
- **Temp: 5-30°C (41-86°F)**
- **Keep cool and dry in winter**

Echinopsis species have possibly the most beautiful flowers of any desert cacti, and among the most colourful are the hybrids developed in Paramount, California.

'Orange Glory' is a particularly beautiful Paramount hybrid. The flowers appear in summer and are a deep glowing orange, a colour not found in pure echinopsis species. Another Paramount hybrid to look out for is 'Peach Monarch', with several long-tubed, peach-pink flowers adorning each plant in early summer.

Echinopsis plants are easy to grow, in either a loam-based or soilless potting mixture. They are greedy plants, so repot every year. Provide strong light to stimulate bud formation.

A few offsets are formed on young plants; these may be left on if a large specimen is desired, or removed for propagation.

To encourage bloom:
When flower buds form feed with a high-potassium fertilizer.

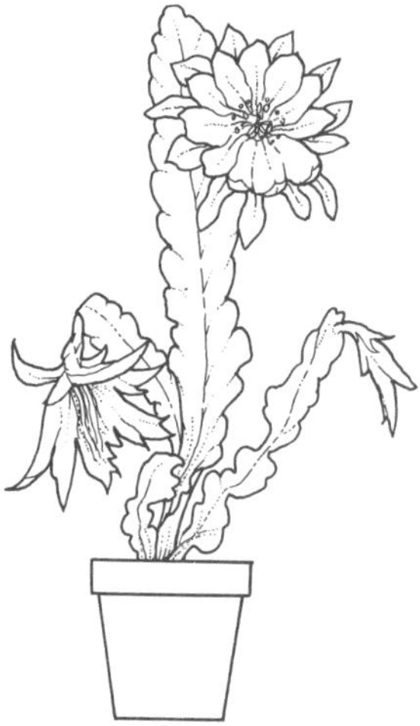

Encyclia cochleata

(Cockleshell orchid)

- **Shade from direct sun**
- **Temp: 10°C (50°F) min.**
- **Evergreen/slight rest**

A subject for the cool house, this South American species produces flattened pear-shaped pseudobulbs about 18cm (7in) tall. The flowers resemble the shape of an octopus in water, with their thin green sepals and petals which droop down below the rounded, dark purple lip.

Several flowers are produced at a time in succession on a flowering spike which, on a large mature plant, can continue flowering for up to two years. Such is the vigour of this species that this is no way impairs its new growth, with the result that two years' flower spikes can be in flower at the same time.

It is one of the few orchids that can be repotted while in bloom. This will be necessary when the new growth has started in the spring. The old leafless pseudobulbs can be removed for propagation. When potted up singly they will readily develop new growths.

To encourage bloom:
Do not overwater. 47▸

Epiphyllum 'Ackermannii'

(Orchid cactus)

- **Partial shade**
- **Temp: 5-27°C (41-81°F)**
- **Keep almost dry in winter**

Epiphyllums (also known as Epicacti) are among the most un-cactus-like cacti and are often grown by plant lovers who profess no interest in conventional cacti. Nevertheless, they are true cacti, but living naturally in tropical rain-forests rather than in the desert. Plants normally cultivated are hybrids between the various wild species and other cacti; such plants are hardier and have more colourful flowers. 'Ackermannii' is a typical example and is one of the oldest in cultivation, but its flowers have not been surpassed in beauty of colour. They are about 8cm (3.2in) across and brilliant red, but not perfumed. The blooms appear along the notched edges of the stems and may last for several days.

You can grow epiphyllums in a standard houseplant mixture, but if you add extra peat or leafmould to it, this is beneficial. Also, good drainage is important.

To encourage bloom:
Feed with high-potassium fertilizer when in bud and flower.

Episcia cupreata

(Flame violet)

- **Good indirect light**
- **Temp: 16-21°C (60-70°F)**
- **Keep on the dry side**

This is an attractive plant that grows in a pendulous fashion and looks good in small hanging pots. Leaves are an attractive greyish silver and green, and flowers, though small, are of brilliant red colouring and appear for many months in the middle of the year. Where growing conditions are to their liking, these plants can be grouped in hanging baskets of reasonable size to make a splendid feature in a room.

Good light is essential, but strong, direct sunlight should be avoided. In terms of temperature there is little to worry about in the summer, but the winter temperature should not drop below 16°C (60°F). Plants need to be potted with a peaty mixture.

In winter it is important to give water sparingly and only when it is really needed by the plant. Winter feeding is not necessary, but plants will benefit from regular applications at other times.

To encourage bloom:
Provide adequate humidity. 48▸

Episcia dianthiflora

(Lace flower)

- **Light shade**
- **Temp: 13-18°C (55-65°F)**
- **Keep on the dry side**

A delightful plant, *E. dianthiflora* has small rosettes of green leaves and produces mis-shapen tubular flowers, white in colour with lace-like, ragged edges to the petals. Growth hangs perpendicularly on stems that will become firm as they age, which makes this one of the best natural trailing plants for indoors.

Avoid excessively wet conditions; aim to give the potting mixture a good watering and allow it to dry quite appreciably before repeating. If plants are growing in hanging pots with drip trays attached it is important to empty these trays an hour or so after watering to ensure that the soil does not become too saturated. Feed established plants occasionally, but do not overdo it; pot on only when the plants are very well rooted. Raise new plants from the rosettes of leaves.

To encourage bloom:
Provide adequate humidity. 48▸

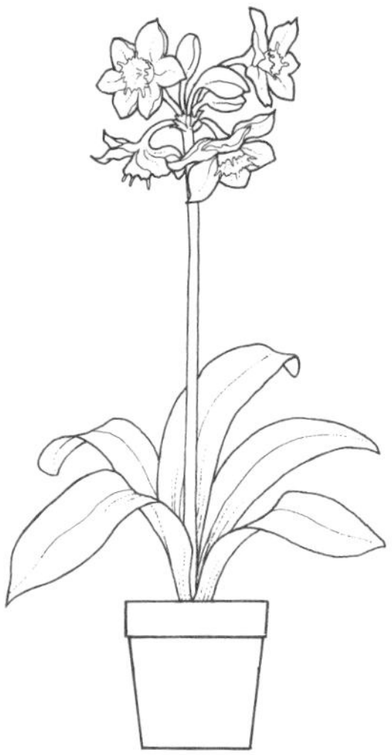

Erica

(French heather; Heath)

- **Good light**
- **Temp: Below 16°C (60°F)**
- **Keep moist**

There are numerous types of ericas, or heathers as they are more commonly known, but for the most part they will develop into neat mounds of needle-like foliage with colourful flowers appearing throughout the year. Individual varieties produce their blooms over a period of weeks, but from a well-chosen collection you could get flowers throughout the year, even in winter.

Almost all the ericas that grow outside will also do very well in large shallow containers. They should be periodically clipped to retain their shape and can spend most of their time on the patio out of doors, being brought in while in flower. In the home these plants require the lightest and coolest location for a long life. Following the flowering period, transfer the plants to the patio and trim any untidy growth.

To encourage bloom:
Keep cool and bright.

Eucharis grandiflora

(Amazon lily)

- **Good indirect light**
- **Temp: 13-18°C (55-65°F)**
- **Keep dry when resting**

Grown from bulbs placed one to a 13cm (5in) pot, these are indeed exciting plants to grow, both indoors and in a frost-protected greenhouse, where they should be placed in good light but not full sunlight. The plant's broad green leaves are pleasing enough in themselves, but it is not until the creamy white flowers appear that the full beauty of this easy-care plant is appreciated.

Following flowering and natural dying down of the foliage it is essential that the plant be kept very dry and allowed to rest in a cool, dry place until new growth is evident, when watering can begin again in the normal way. Ideally, resting plants should be placed on their sides under the greenhouse staging. If treated in this way plants will be more inclined to produce their exotic flowers. Feed occasionally with liquid fertilizer when in leaf.

To encourage bloom:
Observe rest period. 65▸

Above: **Eucharis grandiflora**
Bright white glistening flowers and large dark green leaves combine to display nature at her best. Highly recommended for indoor gardens. The blooms are fragrant. 64▸

Left: **Exacum affine**
Not spectacular but certainly worth space in the indoor garden, Exacum has small fragrant flowers that may last well into the winter months. 82▸

Right: **Euphorbia milii**
The stems of this small shrub are covered in sharp prickles. Bright red bracts give the plant appeal. 81▸

Below: **Euphorbia pulcherrima**
This popular indoor plant is tough to beat for midwinter colour with its large showy bracts in shades of red, pink or white. This photograph shows several individual plants grouped together, each one of which produces bracts of a single colour. The bracts do not change from white through pink to red as the plants become fully grown. 82▸

Above: **Fuchsia 'Snowcap'**
Lovely plants with pendent flowers in various colours, fuchsias can be difficult but worth the trouble. Highly regarded as an indoor plant where growing conditions are suitable. 83▸

Right: **Freesia**
Available in many different colours, the graceful flowers of freesias are exquisitely scented. Beautiful for indoor display as cut flowers. 83▸

Below: **Gardenia jasminoides**
Very popular but difficult to bloom, with lovely scented white flowers. 84▸

Above:
Gymnocalycium mihanovichii 'Hibotan'
Cultivars of the pretty globular cactus are available in a variety of colours, but without chlorophyll they cannot survive on their own. They are grafted onto a green rootstock. The original species (left) is green and will flower on its own roots. 85▸

Above right:
Gloriosa rothschildiana
A fine tuberous plant with narrow leaves and showy orange, crimson and yellow flowers in summer. Start the tubers in spring. 84▸

Right: **Guzmania lingulata 'Minor Orange'**
A fine small bromeliad, this guzmania has a rosette of apple green leaves. A spectacular orange inforescence that lasts for several months puts this plant high on anyone's list for indoor colour. 85▸

Above: **Heliotropium hybrid**
The fragrant purple flowers of heliotrope bloom from spring to autumn. A dependable plant for the beginner to grow with confidence. 87▸

Below: **Heliconia angustifolia**
Very tropical in appearance, with orange bracts and green-white flowers. Different, and one of the best heliconias for indoors. 87▸

Above: **Haemanthus katharinae**
Once coaxed into bloom, the rewards are certainly worth the effort – the bright red flower head will certainly dazzle the eye. Needs plenty of sun to thrive indoors. 86▸

Above: **Hibiscus rosa-sinensis**
Many varieties grow and bloom indoors, with large colourful flowers. Try in tubs in a garden room. 88▶

Left: **Hyacinthus orientalis**
The very fragrant packed flower spikes make hyacinths an indoor favourite. Varieties are available in many colours. Take your pick from white, yellow, pink or blue. 90▶

Above right: **Hoya bella**
This fine plant has waxy clusters of fragrant white-purple flowers that perfume a room. Especially rewarding in hanging baskets. 89▶

Right: **Hoya australis**
Blooming in summer or autumn, this plant from Australia has small white waxy flowers with a tinge of red around the centre. Grow potbound. 89▶

Above: **Hypocyrta glabra**
Known for their goldfish shaped orange flowers, hypocyrtas are compact plants; the shiny leaves of this species make it handsome even when not in bloom. 91▸

Left: **Impatiens wallerana**
One of the easiest houseplants to grow, busy Lizzie produces red or white flowers throughout the year. Easy tc propagate from cuttings. 92▸

Right: **Hydrangea macrophylla Lacecap type**
Shrubby plants with fine clusters of pink, blue or white flowers; a traditional and very successful houseplant for cool rooms. 91▸

Above: **Ixia hybrid**
The rich crimson blooms of the corn lily provide dazzling indoor colour in late spring. Very free-flowering, but it must be kept cool all the time. 92▸

Right: **Jacobinia carnea**
A handsome Brazilian plant with dark green leaves and plumes of pink flowers. Nice amenable plant for a sunny window. Easy to grow. 93▸

Above: **Ixora 'Peter Rapsley'**
An undemanding plant with upright growth and beautiful clusters of red flowers in early summer. A charming plant, not to be missed. 93▶

Above: **Kalanchoe pumila**
Here is a plant that can take almost any indoor situation and survive – with beauty. Flowers are reddish purple, small leaves oval. 95▶

Above: **Kohleria amabilis**
A gesneriad with lovely green leaves and beautiful pink flowers in spring and summer. Makes a fine show in a hanging basket, but needs warm and humid conditions to thrive. 95▸

Euphorbia fulgens

(Scarlet plume)

- **Good light**
- **Temp: 16-21°C (60-70°F)**
- **Keep on the dry side**

This is an untidy sort of plant that produces small but brilliantly coloured scarlet flowers in early spring – a good time for indoor flowering plants when there is so little colour around. Like the more common *E. pulcherrima* (poinsettia) the bright scarlet flower is in fact a bract that surrounds the smaller and insignificant central flowers.

New plants can be grown from tip cuttings about 10cm (4in) in length, which should be inserted in clean peat moss and kept at a temperature not less than 21°C (70°F). The sap of this euphorbia can cause skin irritation, so gloves must be worn when the stem of the plant is being cut. Feed occasionally. Avoid both wet and cold conditions.

Plants will grow to a height of about 120cm (4ft) in ideal conditions. Check regularly for mealy bugs which may infest this plant if it is grown in too dry an atmosphere.

To encourage bloom:
Keep plant in bright light.

Euphorbia milii var. splendens

(Crown of thorns)

- **Full sun**
- **Temp: 10-30°C (50-86°F)**
- **Keep slightly moist in winter**

This delightful little shrub, only slightly succulent, is very popular as a houseplant, and deservedly so, as it is more suited to a well-lit living-room window in winter than to the average colder greenhouse, where it will certainly lose its long leaves, and probably its life also!

The plant's great attraction is its brilliant scarlet flower-like bracts, about 1.5cm (0.6in) across, produced freely in spring and summer. There is also a yellow version.

If the stems become too long, encourage more bushy growth by cutting them down to size; this also provides ample cuttings for spare plants. Keep any sap away from your eyes or mouth. Let the pieces dry for a few days and pot up; they should root fairly easily in spring and summer. Grow this euphorbia in any good loam- or peat-based potting mixture, and water freely in spring and summer.

To encourage bloom:
Provide full sunshine. 67▸

Euphorbia pulcherrima

(Christmas flower; Poinsettia)

- **Good light**
- **Temp: 16-21°C (60-70°F)**
- **Keep moist and fed**

This plant with its bright red, creamy green, or pink-coloured bracts is by far the finest of all winter-flowering indoor plants. The end of autumn to early winter is their natural flowering time and, given reasonable care, they will continue in colour for many months.

Avoid temperatures below 16°C (60°F) and be careful to water plants and allow them to dry reasonably before repeating. Feeding should never be to excess – weak liquid fertilizer can be given each week, and this should be sufficient for most plants.

To get plants to flower for a second year indoors ensure that only natural daylight is made available from early autumn until early winter. When not in flower, prune to shape.

Tip cuttings can be taken from new side-shoots after the bracts have dropped. Wash the poisonous latex from the cut end and insert in an equal mix of peat and sharp sand.

To encourage bloom:
Be sure a dark period is given. 66▸

Exacum affine

(Arabian violet; German violet; Persian violet)

- **Good light**
- **Temp: 13-18°C (55-65°F)**
- **Keep moist and fed**

In small pots on the windowsill there can be few prettier plants than *E. affine,* which has glossy green foliage and scented lavender-blue flowers. An added bonus is that, if old flowerheads are removed, the plant will continue in flower for many months from midsummer onwards.

In common with almost all flowering plants this one should have a very light location in which to grow. But very strong sunlight must be avoided, particularly when it is being magnified by window panes. Besides being a good individual plant *E. affine* is an excellent subject for including in mixed plant arrangements. Keep established plants moist and fed. New plants should be raised annually from seed.

New varieties with bright blue and with white flowers are available, so extending the colour range of this delightful plant.

To encourage bloom:
Keep plants humid and brightly lit, and pick off flowers as they fade. 66▸

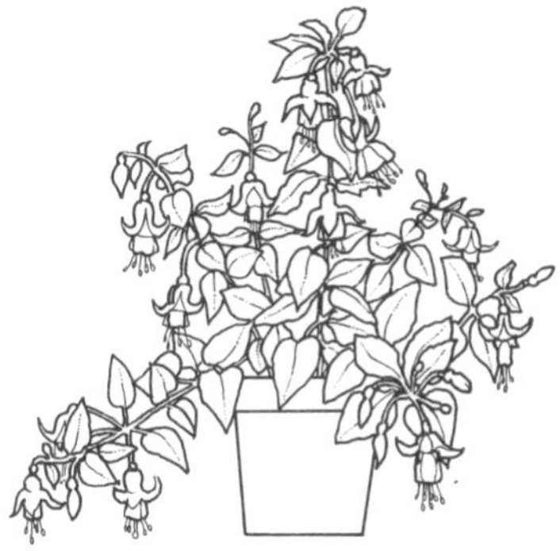

Freesia

- **Good light**
- **Temp: 10-16°C (50-60°F)**
- **Moist; dry in winter**

Among the most fragrant of all flowers the freesias are available in many wonderful colours, and will fill the entire room with their scent. The small bulbs belong to the iris family, and should be planted in loam-based houseplant soil in the autumn. Plant just below the soil surface and place bulbs almost touching in a shallow pot about 18cm (7in) in diameter. Pots are then placed in a cool, sheltered place (an unheated greenhouse, for example) in good light to establish. Once under way they can be transferred to a warmer location to develop their flowers, and placed on a light and cool windowsill indoors when blooms are present. Freesias are excellent as cut flowers, too.

Keep moist while in leaf; feeding is not normally necessary as bulbs are planted in fresh soil each autumn. Dry off and store bulbs after flowering.

To encourage bloom:
Keep cool and brightly lit. 69▸

Fuchsia

(Lady's eardrops)

- **Sunny location**
- **Temp: 13-18°C (55-65°F)**
- **Keep moist, and feed well**

Given proper care this is possibly the best of all the potted plants as far as flower production and length of season goes. They can produce blooms from spring until early autumn with a seemingly never-ending display. But they can also be extremely disappointing for the indoor plant grower, as fuchsias must have maximum light if they are to flower as well as they might. It will often mean that plants are happier and produce more flowers if grown on the windowsill outside the window rather than the sill in the room. In poor light indoors it will be impossible for plants to produce flowers.

A loam-based potting mix is essential for healthy plants. Keep them moist and well fed while in active growth, and prune back severely in the autumn when they begin to lose their summer sparkle.

To encourage bloom:
Mist spray plants regularly to maintain a high humidity. Provide as much light as possible. 68▸

Gardenia jasminoides

(Cape jasmine)

- **Light shade, no sun**
- **Temp: 18-21°C (65-70°F)**
- **Keep moist**

These are shrubby plants with small oval-shaped green leaves that will have a marked tendency to take on chlorotic yellow colouring if conditions are not to the liking of the plant. They are difficult plants to care for, needing a temperature of not less than 18°C (65°F), a lightly shaded location, and careful watering and feeding. Rain water is preferable to tap water and it will benefit plants if the foliage is misted over with water when the atmosphere tends to be dry. Frequent weak feeding will be better than giving occasional heavy doses. Use an acid-type fertilizer and pot the plants in an acid or peat-based mixture.

But, in spite of the problems, the gardenia is well worth trying to raise, as there are few flowers that can match its heavy, overpowering scent. Flowers are creamy white and up to 10cm (4in) across.

To encourage bloom:
Keep plants in constant warmth and high humidity as flower buds form.

Gloriosa rothschildiana

(Glory lily)

- **Good light**
- **Temp: 13-18°C (55-65°F)**
- **Keep moist, but dry when dormant**

These showy plants have glossy leaves and upright habit. They produce a wealth of exotic flowers during the summer months in orange and yellow with a crimson edge.

Plants should be started from tubers; these should go one to an 11.5cm (4.5in) pot in peaty soil and later be transferred to pots of about 18cm (7in) in diameter when the smaller pots are well filled with roots. Use a loam-based mixture at this stage and put at least three of the contents of the smaller pots into the larger one, so that a good show is provided when the plant comes into flower.

It is also wise to place three or four 150cm (5ft) canes around the edge of the pot to which plants can be tied as they develop. Rest tubers during winter in a cool dry place.

To encourage bloom:
Keep plants moist when growing actively but be sure to provide dry dormant period. 71▸

Guzmania lingulata

(Orange star; Scarlet star)

- **Good light**
- **Temp: 13-18°C (55-65°F)**
- **Keep on the dry side**

Belonging to the fine bromeliad family, there are a number of guzmanias that can be found in the quest for new plants to add to the houseplant collection, and all of them will be very easy to manage indoors.

The growing habit is that of most bromeliads – the plant forms a stiff rosette of leaves that protrude from a short and stout central trunk. Overlapping leaves make a natural watertight urn, which must be kept filled with water. However, it is advisable to empty the urn and refill with fresh water periodically. Rain water is preferred but try to avoid getting the soil in the pot too wet. Impressive orange-scarlet bracts develop on short stems from the centre of the urn during winter. New plants can be started from offsets.

Bromeliads should be grown in a free-draining mixture; equal parts of a loam-based medium and peat will be ideal. Alternatively, use a prepared bromeliad mix.

To encourage bloom:
Grow in bright filtered light. 71▸

Gymnocalycium mihanovichii 'Hibotan' *(Chin cactus)*

- **Partial shade**
- **Temp: 10-30°C (50-86°F)**
- **Keep dryish in winter**

Looking something like a tomato on a stick, this cactus, sometimes also called 'Ruby Ball', is certainly unusual. It was first developed in Japan. Some cacti suppliers incorrectly call it the 'everlasting flower'. But the top is no flower, simply an abnormal version of *G. mihanovichii*, lacking chlorophyll. Consequently this novel cactus must always be grown grafted.

A tender jungle cactus, hylocereus, identified by its three-cornered stem, is most often used as a grafting stock; unless you can keep a winter temperature of at least 10°C (50°F), it is better to re-graft onto something tougher, such as a trichocereus. Otherwise treat 'Hibotan' as a houseplant, for which it is ideally suited. You may be rewarded with attractive white or pink flowers. Use a potting mixture of three parts of a standard material and one part of sharp sand or perlite, and be careful never to overwater.

To encourage bloom:
Observe winter rest period. 70▸

Haemanthus katharinae

(Blood flower; Blood lily; Catharine wheel)

- **Good light**
- **Temp: 16-21°C (60-70°F)**
- **Keep moist, dry when dormant**

Haemanthus are grown from bulbs planted to a little over half their depth in a free-draining, loam-based potting mixture. To help with the drainage incorporate a good amount of sand and ensure that some drainage material – pot shards, for instance – is placed in the bottom of the pot before adding the mixture.

Water sparingly until green leathery leaves appear, then more freely, but never to excess. On stems about 30cm (12in) in length the plant bears globes of small orange-red flowers in late spring. Place single bulbs in pots of 13cm (5in) diameter and continue growing the plants in the same potting mixture for several years to get the best results. When foliage naturally colours at the end of the summer allow the soil to dry completely and store the bulb in a warm dry place.

To encourage bloom:
Grow in bright light when active and repot only when roots appear on the surface of the soil. 73▸

Hedychium gardnerianum

(Kahli ginger)

- **Good light**
- **Temp: 16-21°C (60-70°F)**
- **Keep moist, and feed well**

These plants of the ginger family (Zingiberaceae) can be grown by dividing the rhizomes in the spring and planting them independently. Once under way plants will grow apace and in time will require containers of about 25cm (10in) diameter. Once established, these plants need regular feeding. Lemon-yellow flowers are produced in summer on stems that may be 120cm (4ft) or more in length. Immediately after flowering, these stems should be cut down.

Where the climate permits, the plants in their pots can be placed out of doors during the summer months. They make excellent terrace plants when in decorative containers. Water freely in summer, but plants must be brought indoors before the weather turns cold and wet.

To encourage bloom:
Provide plenty of sunshine and keep plants moist and fed.

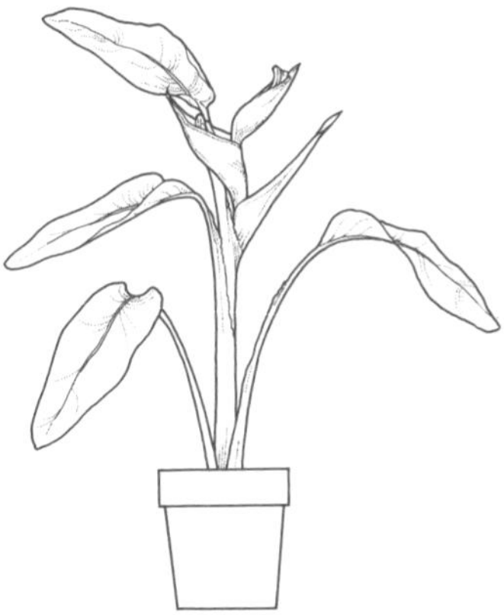

Heliconia angustifolia

- **Good light**
- **Temp: 13-18°C (55-65°F)**
- **Keep moist; dry winter rest**

A native of Brazil and belonging to the same family of plants as the banana, *H. angustifolia* flowers during the summer months. Flowers are white and green in colour with scarlet spathes and can be quite dramatic against glossy green foliage.

New plants can be started by dividing roots in early spring and planting them in 13cm (5in) pots filled with a loam-based potting mixture. These are hungry plants and will quickly exhaust the goodness contained in an all-peat growing medium.

Plants should be freely watered during the summer months and will benefit from having the foliage misted with water at regular intervals each day. Feed well during these active months. No water is required during the winter months when the plants are resting.

To encourage bloom:
Grow in bright light and give dry winter rest. 72▸

Heliotropium hybrids

(Cherry pie; Heliotrope)

- **Sunny location**
- **Temp: 13-18°C (55-65°F)**
- **Keep moist and fed**

An old-fashioned plant that is as popular as ever, being easy to care for and free-flowering both in the garden and on the windowsill indoors.

New plants may be grown from seed sown in the spring, or from stem cuttings inserted in a peaty houseplant mixture. Cuttings of non-flowering pieces about 10cm (4in) in length can be taken at any time during the summer months. Once under way it is advisable to remove the growing tips of the young plants to encourage branching. Standard plants can be grown, but this will take some time and entails growing a single stem that should be stripped of all foliage except for the topmost cluster of branches. These plants must be protected from winter cold.

The attractive flowers appear in the summer and, depending on the variety, are violet, lavender or white in colour. The plants are generally disease-free.

To encourage bloom:
Water freely while in growth. 72▸

Hibiscus rosa-sinensis

(Chinese hibiscus; Chinese rose; Rose mallow)

- **Sunny location**
- **Temp: 13-18°C (55-65°F)**
- **Keep moist and fed**

These shrubby plants are widely dispersed throughout the tropics. They make fine indoor plants for the very light window location. Special growth-depressing chemicals are used to keep the plants short and compact, and to induce abundant blooms.

Trumpet flowers in numerous colours remain open for only a single day, but they are constantly being renewed from new buds during the summer months. It is important that plants have the best possible light and that the soil does not dry out during spring and summer; less water is required in winter.

Harsh pruning is not necessary, but in the autumn plants may be trimmed back to better shape. In the spring, when new growth is evident, pot the plants on into slightly larger containers. Use a loam-based mixture for best results.

To encourage bloom:
Keep in constant temperature; sudden changes may cause buds to drop. Provide ample sunshine. 74▸

Hippeastrum hybrids

(Amaryllis)

- **Good light**
- **Temp: 13-18°C (55-65°F)**
- **Keep moist; dry winter rest**

Production of high-quality hippeastrum bulbs is one of the great skills of the more specialized commercial growers. But once matured, and in good light, these bulbs will produce their exotic trumpet flowers in a range of many colours. These are carried on stout stems 90cm (3ft) or more in height.

Bulbs can be purchased complete with their pots and growing soil and simply require the addition of water to start them growing. They should be kept moist but not excessively wet. However, problems can arise in subsequent years as not everyone can manage to get these plants to flower a second time. It helps to continue to feed the bulb and leaves after flowering until such time as the foliage dies down naturally, when the soil should be dried out and the plant stored cool and dry for the winter.

To encourage bloom:
Grow in bright light when active. Observe rest period.

Hoya australis

(Porcelain flower; Wax plant; Wax vine)

- **Good light**
- **Temp: 16-21°C (60-70°F)**
- **Keep moist and fed**

These attractive plants will climb or trail. To climb they will need a supporting frame, and to trail a hanging basket is ideal. The growing tips should be removed to encourage a bushy appearance. However, avoid unnecessary pruning as plants produce their flowers from older rather than new growth.

A loam-based, well-drained potting mixture should be used and the addition of a little charcoal when potting will prevent the mixture becoming sour. Remember to keep plants on the dry side during winter.

New plants can be raised from stem cuttings taken from the previous year's growth and inserted in peat and sand at a temperature of about 21°C (70°F). Or, more simply, trailing pieces of stem can be pegged down during the summer and then cut from the parent plant and potted individually when they have rooted.

To encourage bloom:
Grow in bright light. 75▸

Hoya bella

(Miniature wax plant)

- **Light shade**
- **Temp: 16-21°C (60-70°F)**
- **Keep on the dry side**

When well established and in full bloom there can be few more rewarding plants than *Hoya bella* growing in a hanging container. The small pale green leaves are attached to wiry stems, but it is the flowers hanging in clusters that are the main attraction. Individual flowers have the appearance of exquisitely cut jewels, white in colour flushed with a delicate shade of pink.

For best results use a loam-based potting mixture that incorporates a reasonable amount of sand to ensure good drainage. If the hanging container is provided with a built-in drip tray, then check an hour or so after watering and tip away any surplus water in the tray. Also, check regularly for signs of mealy bug on the undersides of leaves.

To encourage bloom:
Do not prune or move plants in bud. Give winter rest. 75▸

Hoya carnosa

(Wax plant)

- **Good light**
- **Temp: 13-21°C (55-70°F)**
- **Keep moist and fed**

The twining stems and dark green leaves of this vigorous plant are quick to grow but the flowers that sprout from the leaf and stem joints are slow to appear. They are more likely to appear first on mature plants, but the clusters of pendulous pink jewels are well worth waiting for. As with all the hoyas, let the old flowers fall naturally and do not break off the flower stalks as these are the source of the following year's flowers.

This hoya makes a rather untidy basket plant, and is seen to best effect when trained to a framework of some kind. In this respect the plant is well suited to a heated conservatory, where growth can be trained overhead so that the flowers can be admired to full advantage when they appear. Well-draining, loam-based potting mixture is essential. Give frequent checks for mealy bugs in branches.

To encourage bloom:
Maintain good light as buds form.

Hyacinthus orientalis

(Hyacinth)

- **Good light**
- **Temp: 10-16°C (50-60°F)**
- **Keep moist; dry rest**

During the winter there can be few more pleasing sights than a bowl of colourful and fragrant hyacinth flowers. It is essential to purchase bulbs that have been specially prepared to flower at this time, as ordinary bulbs will not succeed. Plant three or more bulbs in a peaty, fibrous mixture during the autumn and then plunge the pot to a depth of about 13cm (5in) out of doors in peat or sand. In these cool conditions the bulbs will develop a sound root system, and plants can be taken indoors when growth is evident. Alternatively, keep the pot indoors in a cool, dark place for several weeks.

In warm rooms flowers will go through their cycle more rapidly, so it is advisable to provide a cool room and, perhaps, bring the plants into the sitting room for special occasions! After flowering, plant in the garden.

To encourage bloom:
Bring into warmth gradually.

Hydrangea macrophylla

Common hydrangea; House hydrangea; Snowball flower)

- **Good light**
- **Temp: 10-16°C (50-60°F)**
- **Keep wet; rest in winter**

The quality of hydrangeas offered for sale as potted plants, like every other potted plant, varies enormously. So, when purchasing hydrangeas ensure that they have fresh green leaves and are not simply a few leaves at the top of a leafless stem with a few ragged flowers attached. Quality plants in many varieties are available, so choose well.

Hydrangeas in pots are offered in the spring and from the moment of acquisition they must be thoroughly watered until the autumn, when plants die back and should be rested overwinter.

Good light and cool conditions are also essential, and when plants have finished flowering indoors they may be placed on the terrace in tubs, or planted in the garden where they should be protected against spring frost. Take stem cuttings in the summer for new plants.

To encourage bloom:
Keep cool and bright. 77▸

Hypocyrta glabra

(Goldfish plant)

- **Light shade**
- **Temp: 16-21°C (60-70°F)**
- **Keep just moist; drier in winter**

With so many plants to choose from, the glossy green succulent foliage and curiously shaped orange flowers make the hypocyrta an excellent plant for rooms offering limited space. Plants can be grown conventionally in pots on the windowsill, or they may be placed in smaller hanging containers. As hanging plants the generally drier conditions that prevail will suit hypocyrtas as they are capable of storing a considerable amount of water in their attractive puffy leaves.

Temperatures in the range 16-21°C (60-70°F) will suit them fine, as will a watering programme that errs on the side of dry rather than wet. These are hungry plants, but an occasional feed will keep them in good trim and help to retain their bright green colouring. New plants can be raised from stem cuttings.

To encourage bloom:
Do not overwater. 76▸

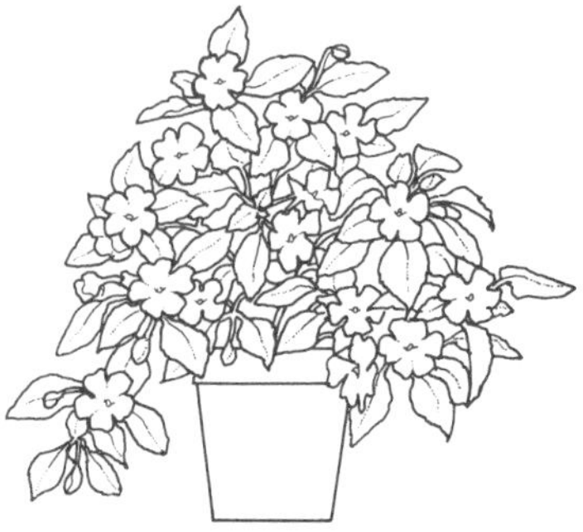

Impatiens wallerana

(Busy Lizzie; Patience plant; Patient Lucy; Snap weed; Sultana; Touch-me-not)

- **Good light**
- **Temp: 10-16°C (50-60°F)**
- **Keep wet and fed**

Capable of attracting a wide assortment of destructive pests, impatiens is, nevertheless, one of the most appealing of all our less costly potted plants.

Good light is essential, and the feeding of established plants is a must. Purchased plants that appear too large for their pots – and this is often the case – should be potted into larger containers without delay. The potting mixture should be loam-based, and the new pot should be only slightly larger than the existing one. In fact, impatiens is one of those odd plants that will tolerate potting more than once in a season. They can develop into splendid plants in time and are also very good in hanging baskets. Remember, though, to inspect frequently for pests and use appropriate remedies without delay.

To encourage bloom:
Allow soil to dry between waterings. Young plants produce flowers most readily – keep taking cuttings. 76▸

Ixia hybrids

(Corn lily; Grass lily)

- **Good light**
- **Temp: 10-16°C (50-60°F)**
- **Keep moist; give winter rest**

The hybrids of *Ixia* come in many delightful colours that will brighten any windowsill. Flowers are fragrant and carried on slender stems.

For a full and pleasing effect try planting five bulbs in a well-draining, loam-based mixture in 13cm (5in) diameter pots in late autumn. Plant the bulbs 7.5cm (3in) deep and place the pots in a dark, cool place until growth is evident. The pots can then be transferred to a cool windowsill indoors. Feeding is not necessary, but the soil must be kept moist, with care being taken to avoid saturation over long periods.

When the foliage begins to die back naturally, cease watering and store the bulbs in a dry, frost-free place until the next season. Do not try planting in the garden: ixias are not hardy out of doors in most temperate climates.

To encourage bloom:
Grow cool and bright once these plants are active. 78▸

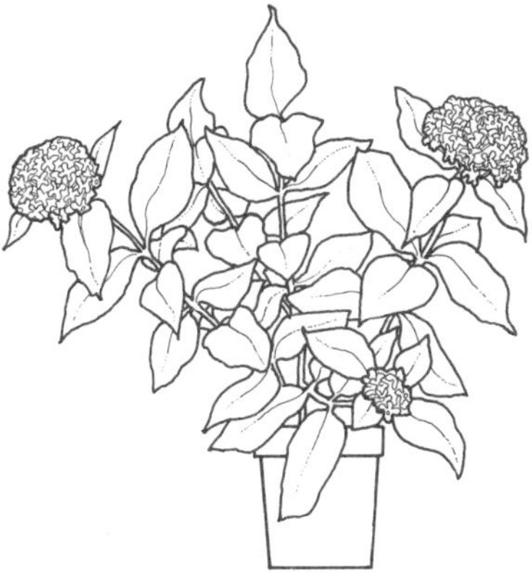

Ixora coccinea

(Flame of the woods; Indian jasmine)

- **Good light**
- **Temp: 16-21°C (60-70°F)**
- **Keep moist; drier in winter**

As the name suggests, *I. coccinea* has brilliant red flowers, but there are also many other colours. All are robust plants growing to a height of about 90cm (3ft).

While in active growth these plants will need regular feeding, but none in winter. The same with watering – ample when plants are in growth, but very little over the winter period. In common with most flowering pot plants these will need a light location in order to obtain the maximum numbers of flowers.

New plants can be grown from cuttings 7.5-10cm (3-4in) long taken in spring and placed in fresh peat at a temperature of about 18°C (65°F). At all stages of potting a proprietary potting mixture is important. It is also essential to ensure that the soil is well drained. Pruning to shape can be done in early spring.

To encourage bloom:
Grow in warm, moist conditions without sudden changes. 79▸

Jacobinia carnea

(Brazilian plume; King's crown)

- **Good light**
- **Temp: 16-21°C (60-70°F)**
- **Keep moist and fed**

This attractive plant has pink flowers that bloom in late summer but there are other varieties occasionally available. Take cuttings of young shoots about 10cm (4in) in length in the spring, using fresh peat and a heated propagator to encourage rooting. Older plants should be cut down to the base after flowering and will flower in subsequent years, but it is often better, if space is limited, to produce new plants from cuttings and to discard the older plant.

While in active growth this vigorous plant will need regular feeding to retain leaf colouring, and ample watering. If an old plant is kept for the following year it will require no feed and little water during the winter. *Jacobinia carnea* is an ideal garden-room plant.

For mature plants use a loam-based potting mixture and repot regularly as the plant grows. Give a winter rest at about 13°C (55°F).

To encourage bloom:
Provide ample light. Take cuttings for vigorous young plants. 79▸

Jasminum polyanthum

(Pink jasmine)

- **Good light, some sunshine**
- **Temp: 10-16°C (50-60°F)**
- **Keep moist and fed**

This climbing plant produces rampant growth in ideal conditions and must have some sort of framework for the spiralling growth to wind around. In winter, plants must be kept in the coolest possible place and will tolerate being out of doors if frosts are not expected.

New plants can be raised very easily from summer-struck cuttings, several cuttings going into a 13cm (5in) pot after they have been rooted in pans or boxes of peat. Use loam-based potting mix, putting the more robust plants in time into 18cm (7in) pots. Provide a fan-shaped framework in the pot so that foliage is well spread, which will in turn display the flowers to best effect when they appear.

The flowers are more white than pink in colour, but the unopened buds are a delicate shade of pink. Feed and water well while active.

To encourage bloom:
Grow cool and bright.

Kalanchoe blossfeldiana

(Flaming Katy; Tom Thumb)

- **Good light**
- **Temp: 10-27°C (50-81°F)**
- **Keep slightly moist in winter**

This succulent is undoubtedly a houseplant, although it can certainly be grown in a greenhouse. Many horticultural hybrids are on the market, as they are popular florists' plants, usually being available in autumn and winter in full bloom. A typical specimen would be up to 30cm (12in) high with wide, thick bright green leaves, but the plants offered for sale are usually smaller. This is predominantly a flowering plant, producing masses of bright red flowers from autumn until spring. The flowers are individually small, but they are clustered in tight heads, giving a brilliant display of colour. There is a yellow-flowered variety.

Never overwater this plant, as the stems are prone to rot off, but never let it dry out completely either. However, in a good, well-drained potting mixture it is easy to cultivate; mix some extra sharp sand or perlite with a standard material to improve the drainage. Take stem cuttings in spring; pot them straight away.

To encourage bloom:
Provide really bright conditions.

Kalanchoe pumila

- **Full sun**
- **Temp: 5-27°C (41-81°F)**
- **Keep slightly moist in winter**

This pretty little plant is ideal for a hanging basket indoors, where it will grow and flower freely in a light window. Of course, it can also be grown in a greenhouse, where its relative hardiness will enable it to survive the lower winter temperature. The slightly thickened leaves are basically pale pinkish-green in colour, but this is almost completely masked by a grey mealy coating, giving the whole plant a delightful pearly-grey appearance. It is very free-flowering, producing masses of dark pink blooms in spring. Although these are individually only about 2cm (0.8in) across, they appear in small groups at the end of quite short stems. The plant is only about 15cm (6in) high.

To grow it in a hanging basket, line a small one with sphagnum moss or coarse peat, well damped, fill with any good potting mixture, and plant the kalanchoe in this. To propagate this succulent, cut off a few stems in spring or summer and pot them up.

To encourage bloom:
Give plenty of light. 79➧

Kohleria amabilis

(Tree gloxinia)

- **Good light**
- **Temp: 16-21°C (60-70°F)**
- **Keep moist and fed**

Plant *Kohleria amabilis* in hanging containers suspended at head level to appreciate fully the attractive bright green foliage and to enjoy the flowers to the full when they appear in late spring and early summer.

However, encouraging plants to produce their attractive pink blooms is not easy. Moist soil, a humid atmosphere and a light position will all help flowering. A further encouragement would be the use of a houseplant food specifically recommended for flowering plants – one that has a fairly high potash content, as opposed to nitrogen. If special fertilizers are unobtainable, try one of the many fertilizers recommended for tomato plants.

Raise new plants by taking cuttings of young shoots in late spring, or by dividing the rhizomes in early spring. Use a peaty soil for potting.

To encourage bloom:
Grow warm and humid. 80➧

Laelia anceps

- **Good light**
- **Temp: 10°C (50°F) min.**
- **Evergreen/dry winter rest**

Some 75 species of *Laelia* have been recorded, almost all from Mexico and the northern parts of South America. Though in appearance both plant and flower are similar to the cattleyas, with which many intergeneric hybrids have been made, it is a delightful genus in its own right, and is favoured by many growers. As with cattleyas, its flower spikes are produced from the apex of the pseudobulbs. The flower spike grows erect to 60cm (2ft) or more and produces two to five flowers, each about 10cm (4in) across. They are pale or deep rose-pink in colour, the lip being a darker hue.

This is an excellent species for the beginner. It can be grown easily in a cool greenhouse or indoors, where it enjoys light conditions. If preferred, it can be grown on a block of wood or cork bark, when an extensive aerial root system will develop.

Propagation is a simple matter of separating the back bulbs and potting them up singly.

To encourage bloom:
Grow cool and bright. 97▶

Lantana camara

(Common lantana; Shrub verbena; Yellow sage)

- **Good light**
- **Temp: 10-18°C (50-65°F)**
- **Water and feed well**

For indoor use it is better to prune lantanas to shape annually in autumn so that a neat and compact shape is maintained. Stems are twiggy and leaves mid-green in colour. The plant will not be difficult to care for if given good light and cool conditions.

Healthy plants in the right surroundings will produce masses of globular flowers throughout the summer months; in poor light, flowers will be less plentiful. Flowers themselves are something of an enigma, as one may see flowers of varying colour on the same plant.

While they are growing more actively in summer, keep plants well watered and fed, but give less water and no feed in winter. Keep a careful check for white on the undersides of leaves, and treat as soon as noticed. This will mean the plant is infested with whitefly.

To encourage bloom:
Provide ample sunshine 98▶

Above: **Laelia anceps**
A large orchid but well worth its space; bears 10cm (4in) pink flowers that last for two months or more on the plant. Very showy in bloom. Needs plenty of sun to thrive. 96◆

Above: **Lilium auratum**
What could be nicer than these fine large white lilies in the home? In pots they add a colourful note to the window garden in summer. 113▶

Below: **Lantana camara**
Lantanas make fine indoor plants, with their yellow and orange flowers and rather odd wrinkled leaves. Good for your brightest window. 96▶

Above: **Lapageria rosea**
The beautiful flowers of this vining plant – here the red with the white-flowered variety – make a stunning show in summer and autumn. Excellent if you have room. 113▶

Above: **Lobivia aurea**
This cactus is not difficult to bloom indoors, and bears colourful, though short-lived, yellow flowers. 114▸

Above right: **Lycaste aromatica**
This popular small orchid with perky yellow flowers is an excellent plant for those new to orchid growing. 115▸

Right: **Mammillaria zeilmanniana**
White and brick red spines decorate this cactus, and flowers are violet-red. Very showy. Ideal for beginners; easy to propagate. 115▸

Above: **Masdevallia coccinea**
Beautiful flowers shaped like kites make this plant look very unlike the orchid it is. Handsome foliage; worth space in cool situations. Provides welcome winter colour. 116▶

Above: **Medinilla magnifica**
And magnificent it is in bloom, with pendulous panicles of carmine flowers in pink bracts. 117▸

Below: **Miltonia Peach Blossom**
A fine small orchid with flat-faced pink flowers, large for the size of the plant. A popular variety. 117▸

Above: **Nerine bowdenii**
This bulbous plant produces a welcome display of attractive pink flowers in autumn. 119▸

Above left: **Miltonia roezlii**
An easy orchid to grow in most situations, this miltonia has white flowers tinged with purple, which last many weeks on the plant. 118▸

Left: **Nerium oleander**
Bushy and big but colourful, with pink, white or red flowers at intervals throughout the summer. 119▸

Right: **Narcissus tazetta 'Paper White'**
Even the novice gardener can bring this lovely white-flowering plant into bloom indoors. Fragrant. 118▸

Above: **Notocactus leninghausii**
A very pretty cactus with soft yellowish spines and bright yellow flowers. Only mature plants bloom. Withstands negligence. 120▸

Left: **Notocactus ottonis**
Very easy to grow and a splendid sight in bloom. It produces many offsets, making propagation simple. Young plants will flower. 120▸

Right: **Odontioda Jumbo 'Mont Millais'**
One of the brilliantly coloured hybrids of Odontoglossum and Cochlioda. A stunning indoor plant. 121▸

Above: **Passiflora caerulea**
Known for its spectacular 7.5cm (3in) flowers of white, blue, and purple, here is nature at her best. A large vine that needs space. 124▸

Left: **Pachystachys lutea**
A shrubby plant with lance shaped leaves and clearly marked veins; overlapping yellow bracts protect the white tubular flowers. 123▸

Right: **Odontoglossum grande**
A most dependable orchid, with large yellow and brown flowers that last for weeks. Sure to bloom. 121▸

Above: **Pelargonium zonale**
Compact clusters of single or double blooms above ring-marked leaves signify these classic geraniums. Ideal for beginners. 125▸

Below: **Pelargonium peltatum 'Rouletti'**
A new bicoloured hybrid. Trailing geraniums, ideal for hanging baskets, prefer a little shade. 125▸

Above: **Pelargonium grandiflorum 'Fanny Eden'**
Large, multicoloured flowers make these hybrids a particular favourite. Like most pelargoniums, they thrive in bright but cool conditions. 125▶

Above: **Pentas lanceolata**
Showy umbels of pink flowers make Pentas a great beauty. A compact and amenable houseplant. 126▸

Left: **Pleione formosana 'Snow White'**
Can't grow anything? Try this exquisite white flowering orchid from China. Sure to please – with lovely 10cm (4in) blooms in spring. 127▸

Lapageria rosea

(Chilean bellflower; Copihue)

- **Good light**
- **Temp: 10-18°C (50-65°F)**
- **Keep moist; drier in winter**

L. rosea can be a most rewarding plant to grow, providing all the right conditions can be met. In an ideal situation the plant will produce elegant funnel-shaped flowers that hang in the most graceful fashion. There are a number of colours available but many people feel that the original crimson form and the white-flowered variety make a stunning combination when grown together.

Grow in a lime-free potting mixture and use rain water when watering. Provide a framework either in the pot or against the wall for the foliage to climb through. Plants flower mainly in the summer and attain a height of about 4.5m (15ft). Provide good drainage and water with care, avoiding hot and dry conditions.

Prune lightly after flowering to take out weak growths. Propagate by seed sown in early spring or by layering strong shoots. Spray against aphids on young shoots.

To encourage bloom:
Maintain lime-free conditions. 99▸

Lilium auratum

(Golden-rayed lily)

- **Good light, some sunshine**
- **Temp: 10-16°C (50-60°F)**
- **Keep moist; dry rest period**

These are not the easiest of plants to manage indoors if they are used as permanent subjects, but they are excellent as temporary plants brought indoors when in bloom.

Bulbs are ready for planting in the autumn and should be planted about half way down a 20cm (8in) pot filled with lime-free peaty mixture. After potting, place the plants in a sheltered spot outside (a cold frame, for example) and cover the pots with a 10-13cm (4-5in) layer of peat. When growth shows through, the plants can be taken into a cool room. Water moderately until the growth becomes more vigorous, then water more freely, using rain water for preference. Stems will require staking. These plants need repotting annually in fresh mixture.

To encourage bloom:
Start in shade and coolness, then grow cool and bright. 98▸

Lithops aucampiae

(Living stone: Stone face)

- **Full sun**
- **Temp: 5-30°C (41-86°F)**
- **Keep dry in rest period**

These little stone-like plants are perhaps the most delightful of all the South African succulents. A large collection of them can be grown in a pan 30cm (12in) square, which makes them ideal for a small greenhouse. Lithops consist of one pair of flat-topped fleshy leaves; the stem is so short as to be invisible when the plant is potted up, and they are often described as stemless. *L. aucampiae* is one of the larger species, with leaves 2.5cm (1in) across; they are a lovely rich brown colour with darker brown dots. The golden flowers appear from between the two leaves in early autumn.

Grow this species in a mixture of half loam-based medium and half sharp sand or perlite. Keep dry all winter. Do not water until the old leaves have completely shrivelled away; this will probably be in late spring. Water on sunny days, and gradually tail off in autumn.

To encourage bloom:
Provide sunshine all year round. Do not overwater.

Lobivia aurea

(Cob cactus)

- **Full sun**
- **Temp: 5-30°C (41-86°F)**
- **Keep dry in winter**

The brilliant lemon-yellow flowers of this lobivia make it outstanding even when placed amongst a group of other beautiful cacti. Its flowers can reach a diameter of 8cm (3.2in) and appear from near the top of the stem during spring and summer. The stem itself is at first globular, later becoming more elongated, and as it reaches a height of only about 10cm (4in), it will not become too large for the collection. There are about 15 ribs along which are groups of spines from 1 to 4cm (0.4 to 1.6in) long.

Any offsets from around the base of the plant may be either left on or removed during spring or summer and, after drying for a few days, potted up for propagation. Either loam- or peat-based potting mixtures may be used for this lobivia, the most important thing being good drainage, which can be ensured by mixing in about one third of extra sharp sand or perlite.

Water may be given freely on sunny days in spring and summer.

To encourage bloom:
Use high-potassium fertilizer. 100▸

Lycaste aromatica

- **Good light**
- **Temp: 10-13°C (50-55°F) min**
- **Deciduous/dry winter rest**

As the name suggests, this species is heavily scented. The bright yellow flowers, 5cm (2in) across, often appear at the same time as the new growth, and are carried singly on a stem about 15cm (6in) long. There may be as many as ten flowers to each pseudobulb.

The plant needs moisture and warmth when in full growth, but take care not to get water on the large, broad leaves, as they tend to develop brown spots if this occurs. Cooler and drier conditions are essential when the plant is at rest and in flower.

Propagation is by removal of the older pseudobulbs, which should not remain on the plant for too many years. It is better to restrict the size of the plant to five or six bulbs, provided they remain about the same size; should the bulbs become smaller, remove all but three or four.

Between 30 and 40 *Lycaste* species are known, including both terrestrial and epiphytic plants.

To encourage bloom:
Keep cool and dry. 101▸

Mammillaria zeilmanniana

(Rose pin cushion)

- **Full sun**
- **Temp: 5-30°C (41-86°F)**
- **Keep almost dry in winter**

This is a very free-flowering mammillaria and the blooms are a beautiful reddish-violet colour; it is one of the few mammillarias of this colour to flower as a young plant. Occasionally a plant has flowers with a double row of petals, and there is also a form with white blooms. The flowering period is early summer.

The stems of this plant are cylindrical, and branch to form multi-headed clumps. Heads can be detached during summer, and used to propagate the plant. Grow in half-pots; a suitable potting mixture is two parts loam- or peat-based medium and one part grit. Water freely and feed every two weeks with a high-potassium fertilizer during spring and summer, allowing it to dry out between waterings. Let it become almost dry during winter. Keep in a sunny part of the greenhouse and inspect for mealy bug; water with insecticide.

To encourage bloom:
Grow in full sunshine; use a high-potassium fertilizer. 101▸

Manettia bicolor

(Candy corn plant; Firecracker plant; Firecracker vine)

- **Good light**
- **Temp: 16-21°C (60-70°F)**
- **Keep moist and fed**

To keep this plant under control requires a framework of some kind through which its twining growth can be trained. Depending on the shape wanted, taller supports can be provided for plants to climb.

New plants can be raised from spring-sown seed, or from cuttings of young growth taken in midsummer and kept warm. When potting, ensure that a liberal amount of sand and charcoal is incorporated in the mixture, which should be loam-based.

Water freely and feed frequently during the growing season, and moderately when growth slows up. Delightful tubular flowers – red with a yellow tip – appear throughout the summer months. Plants can be moderately pruned after they have flowered. During the summer *Manettia* will need protection from strong sunlight.

To encourage bloom:
Provide bright light all year round and keep plants moist and fed when growing actively.

Masdevallia coccinea

- **Shady conditions**
- **Temp: 10°C (50°F) min.**
- **Evergreen/no rest**

This is one of the most fascinating orchid genera, as remarkable for the uniformity of its vegetation as for the diversity of form and colour of its flowers. Three hundred species are recorded, growing mainly in the higher-altitude areas of Mexico, Brazil and Colombia. The structure of the flowers is in contrast to that of many orchids, as the sepals are very large in comparison with the other segments of the flower.

This species produces leaves 30cm (12in) in length, and the flower spikes are often much taller. These bear a single flower of 7.5-10cm (3-4in), with sepals that taper sharply towards the tips. The colour varies from lilac to deep crimson.

Because of the high-altitude conditions of its natural habitat, the cool house with plenty of shade and fresh air during the summer months provides the ideal environment. Masdevallias do not produce pseudobulbs – the thick leaves spring directly from a rhizome.

To encourage bloom:
Keep plants continually moist.

Medinilla magnifica

(Love plant; Rose grape)

- **Light shade**
- **Temp: 18-24°C (65-75°F)**
- **Keep moist and fed**

Native to the Philippines, this plant will be a test for all who are interested in houseplants, but the reward of seeing pink flower clusters suspended from healthy plants will make all the effort worthwhile. Warm conditions, around 21°C (70°F), and a lightly shaded location are essential. Plants must be watered well throughout the year, with slightly less needed in winter.

Pendulous flowers may appear throughout the year, with summer being the most prolific time. The plants have square-shaped stems from which the flowers sprout and develop in the most amazing fashion. Use a loam-based potting mixture to which some peat and leaf mould have been added. Feed when in active growth. To get the full effect of the pendulous flowers place the plant on a pedestal.

To encourage bloom:
Keep in humid conditions. Only mature plants will bloom. 103▸

Miltonia Peach Blossom

(Pansy orchid)

- **Medium light**
- **Temp: 13°C (55°F) min.**
- **Evergreen/no rest**

This is a typical *Miltonia* hybrid produced from the soft-leaved Colombian species commonly known as the 'pansy orchids'. These hybrids come in a wide variety of colours — white, yellow, pink and red. Peach Blossom is one of the most popular varieties with large, plum red flowers, the colour shading to white towards the edges.

This orchid and other similar hybrids should be grown in an intermediate greenhouse or a warm room. Their dislike of cold, damp conditions makes them ideally suited to the drier atmosphere in the home. Watering should be on a continuous basis; never allow the plants to dry out completely. The foliage should not be sprayed and feeding should be applied to the pot when watering. One weak feed every three weeks during the spring and summer should be sufficient.

Repotting should be done when the new growth is showing, which may be spring or autumn.

To encourage bloom:
Maintain stable conditions. 103▸

Miltonia roezlii

(Pansy orchid)

- **Medium light**
- **Temp: 13°C (55°F) min.**
- **Evergreen/no rest**

This extremely pretty plant is one of the soft-leaved Colombian species. It produces the typical neat oval pseudobulbs of the type and these are partially covered by soft, silver-green leaves. The flower spike appears from inside the first or second leaf on the newly completed bulb and carries two to four white flowers. The two lateral petals are painted purple at their bases and the lip has a yellow blotch that spreads out from the centre, or 'mask'. Although this plant is quite rare, supplies should be available from nursery-raised stock.

Although this species likes fairly warm conditions, it should not be allowed to suffer from too high temperatures. The intermediate section of the cool house will suit it. A beginner would find the many superb hybrids that have been raised from this species tolerant and easy to grow in suitable conditions.

To encourage bloom:
Maintain humid conditions. 104▸

Narcissus tazetta 'Paper White'

- **Sunny location**
- **Temp: 10-16°C (50-60°F)**
- **Keep moist; dry rest period**

This is just one example of the many fine bulbs that can be made to flower in pots indoors in early spring, so giving a feeling of spring before its arrival. To succeed, these bulbs have to be thought of in the autumn when they are being sold by retailers. Plant them in shallow pans filled with bulb fibre so that the tips of the bulbs are just poking through the surface of the mixture. After potting, place the planted bulbs in a corner out of doors and cover the pots with about 13cm (5in) of peat or sand, then forget about them!

When the growing tips are showing through the peat or sand surface, move the pots and put them in a cool place indoors. The warmer the place the quicker the bulbs will come into flower, and the shorter will be their life once they have flowered. Avoid excesses of temperature.

To encourage bloom:
Start in coolness and in the dark. Keep fairly cool in light conditions for long flowering period. 105▸

Nerine bowdenii

- **Sunny location**
- **Temp: 10-16°C (50-60°F)**
- **Keep moist; dry in summer**

These bulbous plants are native to South Africa, and most attractive when grown as pot plants indoors or as hardy plants in the garden. Good light and cool conditions are essential needs.

The bulbs are about the same size as those of small daffodils and should be planted five to a 13cm (5in) pot during late summer. Place drainage material in the bottom of the pot then half fill it with loam-based potting mixture. Place the bulbs on this mixture then fill in the remainder of the space with more soil, firming it around the bulbs and leaving the neck of the bulbs exposed. Keep the potting mixture moist. Oddly, these bulbs rest in bone dry condition from early to late summer, when they are best placed on a sunny shelf in the greenhouse. Potting on is seldom necessary. Beautiful pink flowers appear in the autumn before the leaves.

To encourage bloom:
Provide dry rest in summer. Grow in full sun. 105▸

Nerium oleander

(Oleander; Rose bay)

- **Sunny location**
- **Temp: 13-21°C (55-70°F)**
- **Keep moist and fed**

Another fine plant frequently seen in the tropics, and yet equally at home in agreeable conditions indoors. A light and sunny location is essential, and plants should be well watered in summer when in active growth — less is required in winter. The same rule applies with feeding, none in winter, but once or twice each week when producing new leaves.

The semi-double rose-coloured flowers are slightly pendulous, fragrant, and a joy to have about the house. Cuttings of non-flowering shoots can be taken at any time during the summer months. Prepare the cuttings about 13cm (5in) in length and insert them in peaty mixture in modest heat. Be sure to wear gloves when taking cuttings to prevent the sap getting on to your skin. This plant is extremely poisonous if any part of it is eaten. When potting use a loam-based mixture.

To encourage bloom:
Provide plants with as much sunlight as possible all year. 104▸

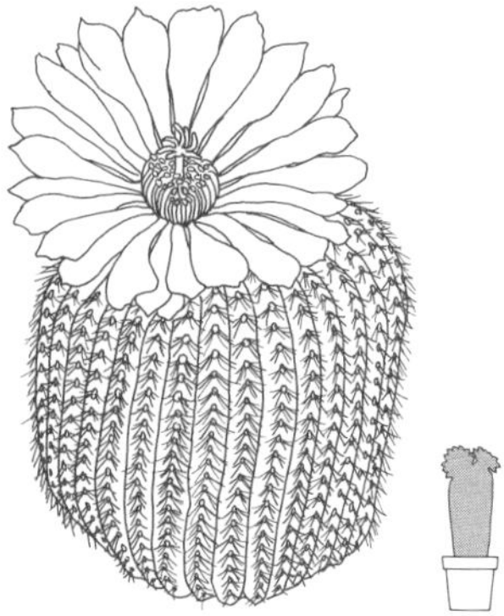

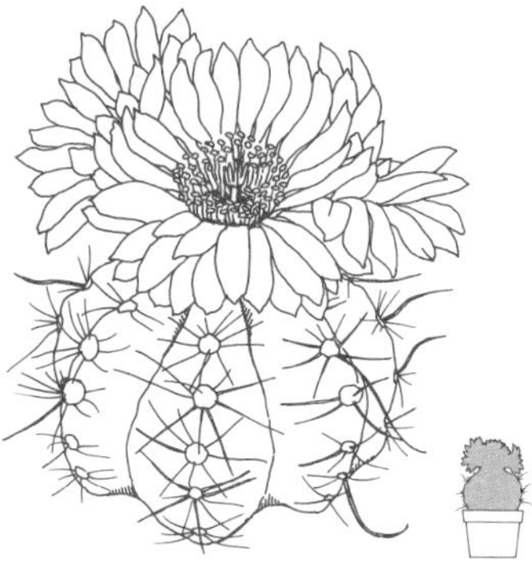

Notocactus leninghausii

(Ball cactus)

- **Full sun**
- **Temp: 5-30°C (41-86°F)**
- **Keep dry in winter**

Notocactus leninghausii is a golden plant that branches and becomes columnar with age. The many close ribs carry soft yellow spines. It is characteristic that the growing centre of this plant tends to be on one side of the stem. The large yellow flowers appear on top of the plant in late summer. Young plants do not flower.

This cactus is not difficult to cultivate; a growing medium consisting of two parts peat-based potting mixture to one part grit, and a sunny position, will ensure a healthy plant. Repot annually. If the plant gets too large or the base of the stem becomes corky, branches may be removed in summer and used for propagation. Water freely during summer, allowing it to dry out between waterings. During flowering, feed every two weeks with a high-potassium fertilizer. Gradually taper the water off in autumn and keep the plant dry during the winter. Watch out for mealy bug.

To encourage bloom:
Give ample sun and winter rest. Only mature plants flower. 106▸

Notocactus ottonis

(Ball cactus)

- **Full sun**
- **Temp: 5-30°C (41-86°F)**
- **Never overwater**

Notocactus ottonis is quite different from other notocacti; it is much smaller, and clusters freely from the base. It is deep green, and the ribs carry slender yellowish spines. Individual heads are about 7.5cm (3in) across. The yellow flowers are about 6cm (2.4in) across.

This notocactus is touchy about watering; to prevent it losing its roots, grow in an open mixture consisting of one part loam-based potting medium to one part grit. Grow it in a half-pot: the cluster looks better, and the roots are not surrounded by large quantities of cold, damp soil. Water freely during spring and summer, always allowing it to dry out between waterings. Feed every two weeks during the flowering period using a high-potassium (tomato) fertilizer. Keep it dry in winter. Place this plant where it will get plenty of light. The main pests are mealy bug and root mealy bug; treat with a proprietary insecticide.

To encourage bloom:
Provide dry winter rest. Grow in small pots. 106▸

Odontioda

- **Good light**
- **Temp: 10°C (50°F) min.**
- **Evergreen/no rest**

Odontiodas result from crossing an *Odontoglossum* with a *Cochlioda*. The most often used cochlioda is *C. noezliana*, which brings its brilliant scarlet colouration to the resulting hybrids. There is a wide range to choose from; new varieties are being raised all the time, and these quickly supersede the older ones. The best way to make a selection is probably to visit a nursery, see the plants in flower, and take advice from the experts.

Odontiodas require cool growing conditions in a position of good light. These plants do not divide or propagate very easily and should be grown on into as large a specimen as possible. Leafless pseudobulbs should not be allowed to outnumber those in leaf and are always better removed when this stage is reached. Regular repotting is essential to ensure the compost remains fresh.

To encourage bloom:
Grow cool and airy. 107▸

Odontoglossum grande

(Clown orchid; Tiger orchid)

- **Light shade**
- **Temp: 10°C (50°F) min.**
- **Evergreen/dry winter rest**

Known widely as the 'clown orchid' due to the clown-like figure represented by the column in the centre of the flower, this is certainly one of the most widely grown in this genus, and popular as a houseplant. The flowers are very large, up to 15cm (6in) across, yellow with bright chestnut-brown markings.

It has hard dark leaves and very tough pseudobulbs, and needs a decided rest during the winter months. During the growing season it needs plenty of moisture at the roots. As the new growth starts to make a pseudobulb towards the end of the summer the flower spike develops. Once flowering is finished and the pseudobulbs have fully matured, water should be withheld until spring, when the new growth appears. The plants need light shade and should be grown in a medium-grade bark compost. They should receive full light in winter.

To encourage bloom:
Observe winter rest period. 109▸

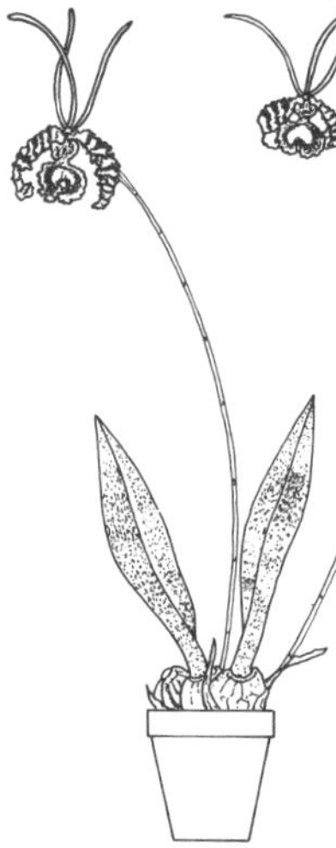

Oncidium ornithorhynchum

(Dancing doll orchid)

- **Good light**
- **Temp: 10°C (50°F) min.**
- **Evergreen/semi-rest**

An extremely showy species from Mexico and Guatemala, this plant has a compact habit and light green pseudobulbs each topped with several thin leaves. The short, slender and arching flower spikes are produced very freely in the autumn and carry the individual flowers on side branches. The colour is a soft rose-lilac with a yellow crest on the lip. They are long-lasting and beautifully fragrant.

Propagation is by division and removal of back bulbs, although the plant is at its best when grown on into a specimen. A very fine rooting system is produced, indicating that a well-drained compost is important. The plant dislikes cold and damp and should therefore not be sprayed overhead or kept too wet at any time. Otherwise, normal cool house conditions will suit it. It is a delightful beginner's orchid of great charm that will do equally well indoors.

To encourage bloom:
Grow cool and bright.

Oncidium papilio

(Butterfly orchid)

- **Good light**
- **Temp: 18°C (65°F) min.**
- **Evergreen/semi-dry rest**

Often referred to as the 'butterfly orchid' because of its resemblance to that insect, this species has flowers that open on the end of a long slender stem and sway in the slightest air movement. Only one per stem opens at any one time, but in succession, so that the plant is in flower for many months. The flowers, which can be up to 13cm (5in) across, are a mixture of chestnut brown and yellow.

The plant has squat pseudobulbs each of which supports a solitary, rigid, reddish-green leaf. The plant grows best on a raft suspended from the roof of the warm house, where it will get that little extra bit of light. It should never be kept too wet at the roots, and does best when kept continually on the dry side, relying upon the humidity in the greenhouse for most of its moisture. It should not be overhead sprayed.

To encourage bloom:
Keep warm and bright.

Pachystachys lutea

- **Good light**
- **Temp: 16-21°C (60-70°F)**
- **Keep moist and fed**

This is a relative of the more familiar aphelandra, but has less vividly marked foliage – the pachystachys having simple mid-green, roughly lance-shaped leaves. However, where the pachystachys scores is in its much longer flowering period and in the fact that healthy plants will produce a far greater number of flowers. Flowers are erect in habit and a rich yellow in colour – or more correctly the bracts are rich yellow, the flowers produced from the bracts being white and tubular in appearance.

Success lies with light, water, and feeding. Avoid direct sun, but keep in the light, and water and feed well. No feeding and less water in winter. Repot annually in a loam-based potting mixture.

Take tip cuttings from the lower branches in spring, dipping the cut end in hormone rooting powder before placing the cuttings in a peat moss and sand mix.

To encourage bloom:
Feed a high-potassium fertilizer. 108▸

Paphiopedilum Maudiae

(Lady's slipper; Slipper orchid)

- **Diffuse light**
- **Temp: 13°C (55°F) min.**
- **Evergreen/no rest**

This is probably the most consistently popular *Paphiopedilum* hybrid in the world. The plant has the grace and beauty found among a few of the species, which have been overshadowed by the heavier, rounded type of hybrids.

The plant is a strong, vigorous grower that can be continually divided without harm to produce further plants. The foliage is beautifully mottled in light and dark green, the leaves are short and rounded. The tall, slender stem carries a single large bloom, distinctively marked in white and deep apple green. Its coloured variety, *Paph.* Maudiae 'Coloratum', shows the same markings on a rich purple ground.

Its ease of culture and long-lasting, long-stemmed blooms, which can be produced twice in one year, have made this hybrid popular for the cut flower trade.

To encourage bloom:
Maintain humidity and warmth but with good ventilation.

Parodia sanguiniflora

- **Full sun**
- **Temp: 5-30°C (41-86°F)**
- **Water with care**

Parodia sanguiniflora, true to its name, has large blood-red flowers. These open in summer, and make a change from the yellow flowers usual in parodias. As a young plant this cactus is globular, but it tends to become cylindrical with age. The numerous spirally arranged ribs carry many brownish spines, some of which are hooked. Some specimens form excessive numbers of offsets to the detriment of flowering. If this happens, restart the plant from an offset. For several years it will flower freely before starting to offset again.

Grow in an open potting mixture, one part loam-based medium to one part grit. Repot annually and inspect the roots for ashy deposits, which indicate root mealy bug; if found, wash off old soil and repot in a clean container. Always water parodias carefully, as they have a tendency to lose their roots if their growing medium becomes excessively wet. Feed with a high-potassium liquid fertilizer when in flower.

To encourage bloom:
Provide sunshine all year round.

Passiflora caerulea

(Passion flower)

- **Sunny location**
- **Temp: 10-16°C (50-60°F)**
- **Keep moist and fed**

This plant is a rampant grower that will need some form of support for the twining growth to attach itself to. Hardy out of doors in agreeable climates, but out or in the plant will give a better show of flowers if the roots are confined to a small space. If allowed a free root run it will tend to produce masses of foliage at the expense of flowers.

Sriking 7.5cm (3in) flowers intricately patterned in blue, white and purple appear in late summer and are followed by colourful orange-yellow fruits.

To do well this plant needs good light, ample watering while in active growth, and feeding with a fertilizer containing a high percentage of potash – a tomato food, for example. When potting is essential, use a loam-based mixture.

New plants can be raised from seed or cuttings in spring.

To encourage bloom:
Provide ample light. Do not use pots larger than 20cm (8in) across, otherwise stems and leaves develop at the expense of flowers.

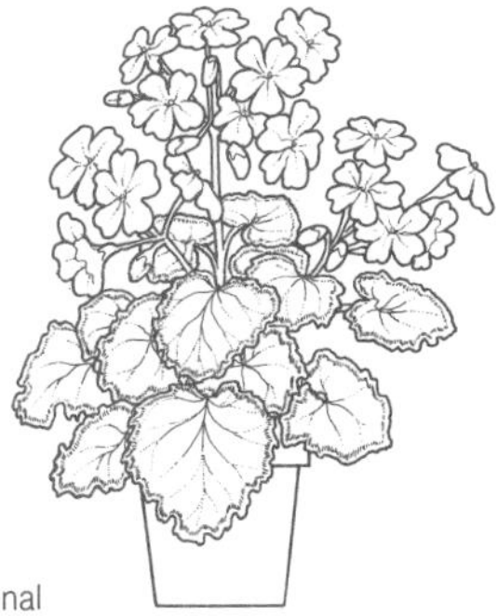

Zonal

Regal

Pelargonium

(Geranium)

- **Sunny location**
- **Temp: 10-18°C (50-65°F)**
- **Keep moist; drier in winter**

Great favourites throughout the world, the pelargoniums come in three principal types: zonals (*P. hortorum* – mainly derived from *P. zonale*); regals (*P. domesticum* – derived from *P. cucullatum, P. fulgidum* and *P. grandiflorum*); and the ivy-leaved forms (*P. peltatum*).

Zontal pelargoniums take their name from the zonal marking of bronze or maroon around the centre of each leaf. The flowers appear over a long period and the plants can grow into shrubs up to 1.8m (6ft) tall.

Regals grow to a maximum height of about 60cm (2ft) and produce impressive, funnel-shaped flowers in many shades from pink to purple. They appear mainly from early spring to midsummer.

Ivy-leaved pelargoniums, with their trailing stems up to 90cm (3ft) long, are ideal for growing in hanging baskets. The compact flowers appear mainly in spring.

There are pelargoniums from these groups that will suit almost any indoor situation, provided it offers ample light and the atmosphere is cool and airy. Use a loam-based potting mixture and water moderately during the warm months. Keep the soil just moist in winter.

Raise new plants from cuttings that have been removed from the parent plant for about twenty four hours before being inserted in a peat-and-sand mixture. Today, however, there is a great emphasis on raising plants from seed, and these do amazingly well.

Ivy-leaved

To encourage bloom:
Feed actively growing plants with a high-potassium fertilizer every two weeks. Grow slightly potbound for profuse flowers. 110-111▶

Pentas lanceolata

(Egyptian star cluster; Egyptian star flower)

- **Good light**
- **Temp: 16-21°C (60-70°F)**
- **Keep moist and fed**

Though not often supplied by growers, this is a fine plant that can be seen in better plant collections. Plants can be started from new shoots about 10cm (4in) in length taken in the spring and placed in a peaty mixture – a warm propagating case will encourage rooting. Once rooted well, the small pots of cuttings should be transferred to slightly larger pots. Place drainage material in the bottom of the new pot before adding loam-based mixture and some grit for improved drainage.

As they develop, remove the growing tips of the young plants. This will encourage a compact habit and prevent the plants growing too tall. Keep the plants in good light and feed regularly and water well while actively growing.

These plants normally flower from early autumn until midwinter, but blooms can appear during the summer months as well.

To encourage bloom:
Maintain bright light throughout the year and allow plants to become slightly potbound. 112▸

Phalaenopsis Hennessy

(Moth orchid)

- **Light shade**
- **Temp: 18-21°C (65-70°F) min.**
- **Evergreen/no rest**

This hybrid is an example of a peppermint-striped phalaenopsis. The plant is very free-flowering, blooming throughout the year, and the branched spikes may bear up to 30 flowers at a time. The individual flowers are 9-12cm (3.5-4.75in) across, white to light pink in basic colour, with red or pink stripes or, in some forms, spots. This hybrid is of fairly recent breeding. From a particular cross, only a percentage of the seedlings will carry the elusive candy-striped markings that are highly valued to increase the variety within the genus.

Phalaenopsis are highly susceptible to damp conditions, when premature spotting of the flowers will occur. A movement of air from an electric fan combined with a drier atmosphere while the plants are in bloom will help to prevent this common problem. The plants will also suffer if given poor light during the winter.

To encourage bloom:
Keep warm and shaded. 129▸

Pleione formosana

- **Good light**
- **Temp: 4.5°C (40°F) min.**
- **Deciduous/dry rest**

About 20 species of pleiones are known and these are found growing close to the snowline of the Himalayas, and also in parts of China and Formosa. The Himalayan species are probably better suited to the conditions of an alpine house, but others do well in the cool section of an orchid house.

The plant consists of a single, squat, roundish pseudobulb, which lasts for only one year. New growth springs from the base of the pseudobulb, and in its early stages produces a flower spike from its centre. This spike bears one or two flowers, up to 10cm (4in) across. The common species has flowers ranging from pure white to pale pinky-mauve. In all variations the broad lip is frilled, and in the coloured forms it is spotted with red-purple.

In the early spring the plants should be taken from their pot, and reset about half-buried in a fine but well-draining compost.

To encourage bloom:
Grow cool and bright. 112▸

Primula malacoides

(Baby primrose; Fairy primrose)

- **Good light**
- **Temp: 10-16°C (50-60°F)**
- **Keep moist and fed**

This is one of the most charming of all the annual flowering houseplants. *Primula malacoides* presents its lovely flowers, in many colour shades, during the winter and spring months of the year and is almost indispensable for that added touch of colour on the sunny windowsill.

Keep the plants in a cool and light place to do well, and at no time expose them to hot and dry conditions. In such conditions there is a much greater chance of the plants being attacked by red spider mites. These can be detected by careful inspection on the undersides of leaves, and should be treated with the appropriate insecticide as soon as they are noticed. Feed regularly to retain leaf colour.

Grow primulas in a loam-based potting mix and keep them moist while they are actively growing and flowering. Discard *Primula malacoides* plants after flowering and raise new plants from seed.

To encourage bloom:
Pick off faded flowers regularly. Give liquid fertilizer when flowering. 129▸

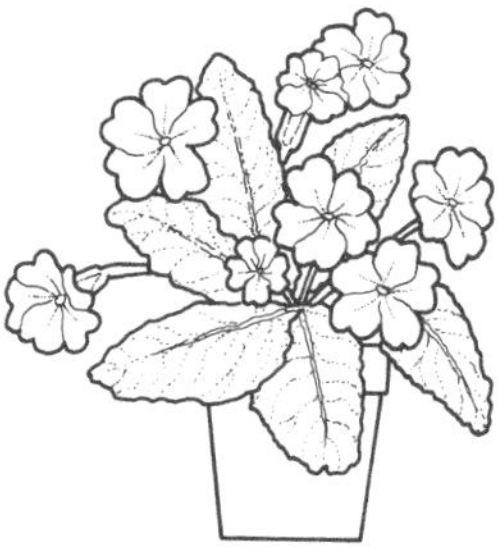

Primula obconica

- **Good light**
- **Temp: 10-16°C (50-60°F)**
- **Keep moist and fed**

These are marvellous plants that seem to flower from one year's end to the next and are very little trouble when it comes to care and attention. Flowers in a variety of colours are more plentiful in winter and spring, but they are likely to be present at almost any time on vigorous plants. Cool, light, and airy conditions are essential. Plants must be kept moist and regularly fed.

The principal drawback with this plant is that it can cause a most irritating rash. Anyone suffering any form of skin problem following the introduction of this plant to the room should immediately suspect and should not actually touch the plant.

To prolong the flowering period give a weak solution of liquid fertilizer every two weeks and pick off fading flowers. This primula can be kept for a second season provided it is kept cool and dry during the summer. In the autumn remove dead leaves and topdress with fresh soil.

To encourage bloom:
Pick off flowers as they fade. Give liquid fertilizer regularly during the flowering period.

Primula vulgaris

- **Good light**
- **Temp: 10-16°C (50-60°F)**
- **Keep moist and fed**

This is now one of the most popular small plants during the winter period. Easily grown from seed sown in the spring, the plants bloom during the winter months. The leaves are pale green and rough in texture, and flowers of many colours are now available; the flowers are infinitely larger than those of a few years ago.

Excellent planted in bowls with other foliage and flowering plants, they will also provide a fine show when a number of plants of different colour are grouped together in a small container.

After flowering indoors, the plants can be put in the garden in a shaded spot to flower the following year.

Keep pot-grown plants in a humid atmosphere while indoors; hot, dry conditions may cause foliage to turn yellow and will cut down the flowering period. Use a loam-based potting mixture and feed every two weeks while the plants are in bloom.

To encourage bloom:
Keep cool with good ventilation.

Above: **Phalaenopsis hybrids**
Now available in yellow, pink, white or 'peppermint' stripes like this P. Hennessy, these are the beauties of the orchid group. 126▸

Right: **Primula malacoides**
Whorls of rose-purple flowers make this an attractive indoor plant. Handsome wavy edged leaves. 127▸

Above: **Punica granatum 'Nana'**
Scarlet red flowers always create a sensation when you grow this miniature pomegranate. 145▸

Left: **Rechsteineria cardinalis**
An overlooked gesneriad, this fine plant has brilliant red 5cm (2in) flowers for many weeks in summer. Ideal size for windowsills. 146▸

Right: **Rebutia calliantha var krainziana**
Tiny and charming, this cactus bears very large red flowers in the summer. Ideal for beginners. 145▸

Above left: **Schlumbergera 'Buckleyi'**
An excellent plant for superb autumn colour and so easy to propagate from simple stem cuttings. A must. 148▸

Left: **Schizocentron elegans**
Blooming at intervals through spring into early summer, this is an easy and colourful pot plant. 147▸

Above and right: **Saintpaulia**
A huge group of favourite plants with varieties in many colours. Also available as miniatures. 147▸

Above: **Smithiantha cinnabarina**
Lush green leaves and handsome bell shaped orange-red flowers make this plant welcome 149▸

Below: **Schlumbergera gaertneri**
Lovely scarlet flowers make this forest dwelling cactus a must for all indoor gardeners. 148▸

Above: **Sinningia**
Many fine hybrids are now available, all with brilliantly coloured flowers for a superb indoor display. 149▸

Above: **Stanhopea wardii**
An unusual orchid with large leaves and waxy flowers borne from the bottom of the plant. Heavily scented with a pleasing fragrance. 151▸

Left: **Solanum capsicastrum**
Prized mainly for its orange fruits rather than its small white flowers, this compact plant brings colour to the windowsill in winter. 150▸

Right: **Spathiphyllum 'Mauna Loa'**
Striking flowers, compact growth and ability to endure neglect make this recommended. 150▸

Above: **Thunbergia alata**
A colourful tropical vining plant that grows well in warm airy conditions. Easy and worthwhile. 153▸

Right: **Streptocarpus hybrid**
If you want dazzling flowers look to the fine streptocarpus hybrids. Blooms come in wonderful shades of violet, pink or white. 153▸

Below: **Strelitzia reginae**
A stunning plant with 15cm (6in) blooms. Needs warmth and space. Spectacular but temperamental. 152▸

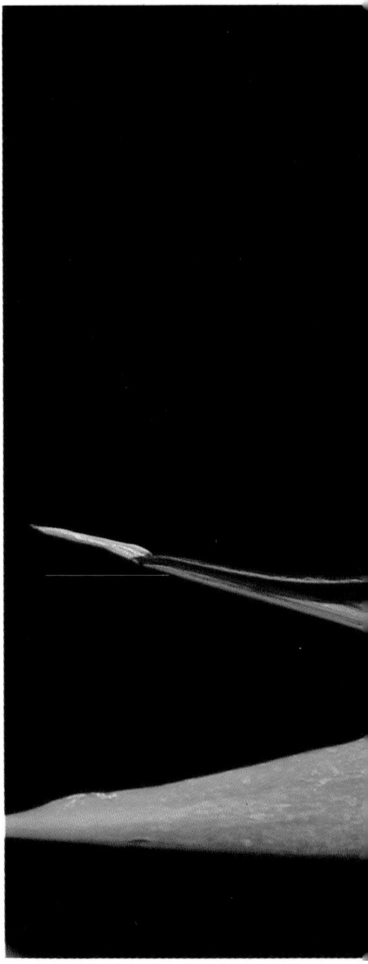

Above: **Vallota speciosa**
A bulbous plant from South Africa, this beauty is easy to grow and quite spectacular in bloom. 155▸

Left: **Tulipa (Triumph type)**
These fine flowers can be forced during the winter to provide welcome colour in the home. 155▸

Above right: **Trichopilia tortilis**
A fine indoor orchid that really does grow and bloom indoors. Unusual flowers with corkscrew petals. 154▸

Right: **Stephanotis floribunda**
It is hard to beat the fragrance of Madagascar jasmine. White star shaped 2.5cm (1in) flowers appear in clusters in summer. 152▸

Above: **Vriesea splendens**
This superb bromeliad offers not only striking foliage but also a long-lasting 'sword' of red bracts. 157▸

Below: **Vanda suavis**
This beautiful orchid from Java and Bali produces fragrant waxy flowers during the autumn. 156▸

Above: **Zephyranthes candida**
Zephyr flowers are pretty and bear graceful blooms during the summer and into the autumn. Flower colour is usually white, but orange and pink varieties are also seen. 158▸

Above:
Zygopetalum intermedium
Another popular orchid, this one bears lovely fragrant green and purple flowers in midwinter. A welcome addition indoors. 158▸

Punica granatum 'Nana'

(Dwarf pomegranate)

- **Good light**
- **Temp: 10-18°C (50-65°F)**
- **Keep moist and fed**

The dwarf pomegranate is a compact and shrubby plant with masses of small green leaves, and it will not be difficult to care for if given good light and cool conditions. Besides the evergreen foliage, the reddish scarlet flowers are also a feature; these are suspended from the plant in similar fashion to those of the fuchsia, but are not quite so plentiful.

If flowers are pollinated with a soft brush when pollen is present there is every chance that small pomegranate fruits will develop; these are not edible, but will be of considerable interest. To preserve a neat appearance it is advisable to periodically prune back any growth that is tending to get out of hand. Keep the soil moist, and feed occasionally, but not in winter.

To encourage bloom:
Provide plenty of sunshine while the plant is actively growing. Provide a rest period during the winter. 130▶

Rebutia calliantha var. krainziana

(Crown cactus)

- **Full sun**
- **Temp: 5-30°C (41-86°F)**
- **Avoid overwatering**

All rebutias are beautiful in the spring flowering period, but this species is outstanding. Each head is surrounded by a complete ring of orange-red flowers. The flower colour in this plant can vary from an almost true red through to a pure orange. The buds are purple.

The individual heads of this clustering cactus are cylindrical, and reach a height of about 10cm (4in). The very short white spines form a neat pattern against the green stem.

This rebutia needs a sunny position to keep it a bright colour and to ensure flowering. Any good potting mixture may be used, either loam- or peat-based. During spring and summer water freely, letting it get almost dry before watering again. When the buds form feed every two weeks with a tomato fertilizer.

Watch carefully for any signs of mealy bug, particularly around the growing point of the stems, where these woolly white pests can fade into the white wool on new growth.

To encourage bloom:
Give plenty of sun. 131▶

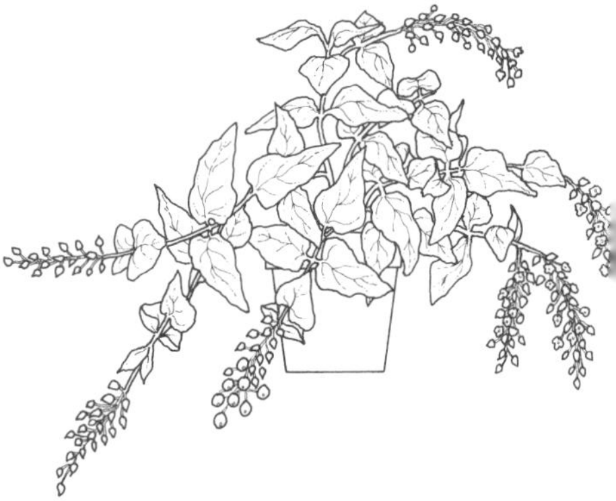

Rechsteineria cardinalis

(Cardinal flower)

- **Light shade**
- **Temp: 18-21°C (65-70°F)**
- **Keep moist and fed**

This is a gesneriad with green velvety leaves that produces flowers of bright red colouring in the autumn. For a neat and colourful plant that is not too difficult to care for, *Rechsteineria cardinalis* (also known as *Sinningia cardinalis*) can be thoroughly recommended.

A temperature of not less than 18°C (65°F) is needed and water must be tepid rather than straight from a cold tap. Exposure to bright light will leach the colouring from foliage and mar the appearance of the plant, so place in light shade. Keep the plant out of draughts.

Water well and feed occasionally during spring and summer when plants are in leaf, but when the foliage dies back naturally withhold water and keep the rhizome bone dry and warm until fresh growth appears.

For new plants take leaf or stem cuttings, grow from seed, or plant pieces of rhizomes.

To encourage bloom:
Give a definite winter rest. 130▸

Rivina humilis

(Baby pepper; Bloodberry; Rouge plant)

- **Good light**
- **Temp: 16-21°C (60-70°F)**
- **Keep moist; drier in winter**

Although an evergreen, these plants will give much better results if fresh material is raised each year. This can be done by sowing seed in the spring for young and vigorous plants to be ready in the summer, or by propagating cuttings. If using the cuttings method, at least one plant must be retained from the previous year so that cuttings can be taken from it for rooting in a heated propagator in the spring.

These neat plants have thin leaves and whitish flowers in the summer to be followed by the further bonus of decorative berries of a bright red colour in the autumn. Keep moist and fed while in active growth, giving less water and no feed to plants retained over the winter period. Check plants regularly for red spider mites and treat promptly.

To encourage bloom:
Raise new plants each year.

Saintpaulia ionantha

(African violet)

- **Good light**
- **Temp: 16-21°C (60-70°F)**
- **Keep moist and fed**

This is by far the most popular flowering plant. There is no particular flowering time, but bloom will be much improved if plants are grown in good light, and this means a light window – no draughts – during the day and under an artificial light in the evening.

Use tepid water and apply it to the surface of the potting mixture ensuring that it drains right through the pot – any surplus accumulating in the drip dish should be removed as it is fatal to allow plants to stand in water for any length of time. Use a standard loam-based potting mixture with some extra peat added. Feed with fertilizer every two weeks.

New plants can be grown from firm leaves taken at any time and placed in a heated propagator or a plastic bag to conserve warmth and moisture. After 6 to 10 weeks tiny plantlets appear at the base of the leaf; these can be separated and grown into mature plants.

To encourage bloom:
Grow slightly potbound. 133▸

Schizocentron elegans (Heterocentron)

(Spanish shawl)

- **Good light**
- **Temp: 16-21°C (60-70°F)**
- **Keep moist and fed**

This compact windowsill plant is ideal for the beginner wishing to have something easy to keep in flower. Neat mounds of green foliage are topped by purplish flowers that are in evidence through the spring and into early summer.

It is best kept in a smaller pot using a loam-based potting mixture, but a keen eye must be maintained for watering and feeding, as smaller pots tend to dry out more rapidly. While actively growing, plants should be fed at every watering with a weak liquid fertilizer. Alternatively, feeding tablets may be placed in the soil as directed by the manufacturer.

New plants can be produced in the autumn by cutting back the foliage of older plants to little more than stumps, then dividing the roots. Alternatively, tip cuttings about 7.5cm (3in) long can be taken at any time and rooted in a mixture of peat and sand.

To encourage bloom:
Provide bright light all year. 132▸

Schlumbergera 'Buckleyi'

(Christmas cactus)

- **Partial shade**
- **Temp: 10-21°C (50-70°F)**
- **Keep slightly moist all year**

There is no doubt that this is the most popular cactus of all and the one most commonly grown, in spite of the fact that many people do not consider it to be a 'true' cactus at all, whatever that means! But it *is* a cactus, a jungle type, needing more warmth and moisture than the desert cacti. The many segments, joined end to end, are true stems (there are no leaves) and the whole plant forms a densely branched bush. Unscented flowers of an unusual shape and about 3cm (1.2in) across, are freely produced in winter at the end of segments; the typical colour is carmine but varieties exist with flowers of various shades of red, pink or even white (never blue).

Use a rich potting mixture with added peat or leaf mould, and water the plant freely when in bud and flower, feeding every two weeks at this time. Reduce the water somewhat after flowering. Propagation from segments is easy.

To encourage bloom:
Give 12-hour days in autumn. 132▸

Schlumbergera gaertneri (Rhipsalidopsis)

(Easter cactus)

- **Partial shade**
- **Temp: 10-21°C (50-70°F)**
- **Keep slightly moist all year**

This delightful little jungle cactus resembles the better known Christmas cactus (*Schlumbergera* 'Buckleyi'). The stem segments are smaller than those of the typical Christmas cactus and are more rounded, with small bristly spines and whilst the flowers are also bright red and freely produced, they are open star-shaped and 3.5cm (1.4in) across. They appear in spring.

Small specimens can be grown in an ordinary pot, but soon the increasing segments will cause the stems to droop, so that eventually a hanging basket is ideal. A well-drained potting mixture is needed, so add about a third part of sharp sand or perlite to a good standard loam- or peat-based material. A fortnightly feed with a high potassium fertilizer in spring will help to ensure a good succession of flowers. Pieces of stem consisting of one or two segments will root readily if removed in spring.

To encourage bloom:
Keep warm and moist. 134▸

Sinningia speciosa

(Gloxinia)

- **Good light**
- **Temp: 13-18°C (55-65°F)**
- **Keep moist; dry rest**

These plants may be acquired as tubers to be grown on, as seed to be sown and reared, or as finished plants from the retailer. Whatever the choice, splendid plants can be owned and admired; they have large, soft green leaves and their trumpet flowers up to 7.5cm (3in) across are produced throughout the summer months. A rosette of leaves develops from the tuber to be topped by almost stemless flowers.

While in leaf plants must be fed only with a high nitrogen fertilizer, but change to a high potash one when flower buds appear. Good light is maybe the most important need of this plant when in flower. Remove dead flowers to encourage new ones. When foliage dies down naturally in early autumn, allow the standard potting mixture to dry completely and store the tuber in a dry and warm place during the winter months.

To encourage bloom:
Give high-potassium feed when buds form. Pick off faded flowers. 135▸

Smithiantha cinnabarina

(Temple bells)

- **Light shade**
- **Temp: 16-21°C (60-70°F)**
- **Keep moist and fed**

These interesting and colourful plants of the Gesneriaceae family can be kept in flower for many months of the year with a planned approach. Initially plants can be raised from seed or cuttings taken in the spring – keep the temperature at around 21°C (70°F) for both. Plants will grow and produce rhizomes and these can be planted at different times: spring planting for flowers in summer; early summer planting for flowers in the autumn; and mid-summer planting for flowers in winter. If a heated greenhouse is available plants can be induced to flower over this extended season to much enhance the indoor plant scene. Once indoors avoid draughts and cold.

Lush green leaves are topped by bell-shaped flowers that are available in many colours. From a packet of seed one would expect to get a good selection of colours.

To encourage bloom:
Feed regularly when active. Observe dormant period. 134▸

Solanum capsicastrum

(Jerusalem cherry; Winter cherry)

- **Sunny location**
- **Temp: 10-16°C (50-60°F)**
- **Keep moist and fed**

These are cheap and cheerful shrubby plants with thin green leaves; they are normally available during the winter. Raised from seed the young plants are established in their pots then placed out of doors in full light and fresh air where they will make sturdy plants. Following the insignificant white flowers plants begin to develop green berries which will eventually turn red and become the plants' most interesting characteristic.

The orange-red berries remain colourful for many months if plants receive adequate light, but will fall at an alarming rate if the light is poor, and this need be for only a very short time. Keep plants moist and regularly fed. It is best to discard the plants after the berries have fallen.

Take care to keep these plants away from children – the attractive berries are poisonous if eaten.

To encourage bloom and fruit:
Mist spray the flowers to encourage the fruits to set. Maintain plants in bright light. 136▸

Spathiphyllum 'Mauna Loa'

(Peace lily; Spathe flower; White flag; White sails)

- **Light shade**
- **Temp: 18-21°C (65-70°F)**
- **Keep moist and fed**

Originally from the Hawaiian Islands, this is truly a very fine plant when grown in conditions that are in tune with its modest demands. The right temperature is one of its most important needs, never less than 18°C (65°F). The roots and the atmosphere surrounding the foliage should be moist, so misting will be beneficial in dry air conditions. Don't overwater, though.

In ideal conditions, plants will grow throughout the year and may produce elegant white spathe flowers at any time. Older plants can be divided to produce new ones and these should be potted into a loam-based mixture containing about 50 per cent peat. Place a layer of broken flower pot in the bottom of the container to improve drainage.

Check the undersides of leaves regularly for red spider mites which may infest the plant in too dry conditions.

To encourage bloom:
Keep warm and humid. 137▸

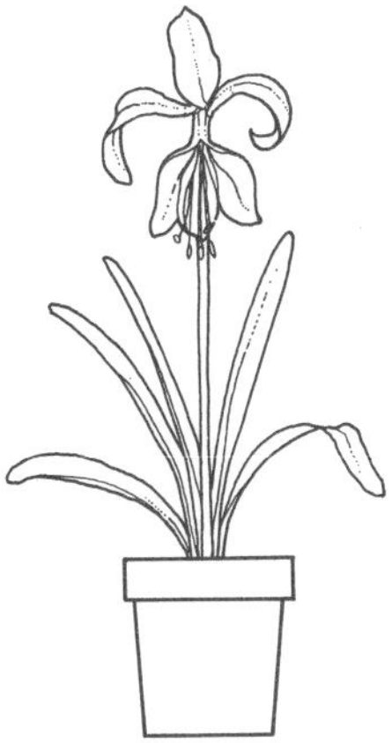

Sprekelia formosissima

(Aztec lily; Jacobean lily)

- **Sunny location**
- **Temp: 10-16°C (50-60°F)**
- **Keep moist; dry in winter**

These are bulbous indoor plants with orchid-like scarlet flowers borne on stems about 50cm (20in) tall in the spring.

The bulbs, which are usually both expensive and in short supply, should be planted with their tips showing in a loam-based mixture that will sustain the plant in the same pot for several years. Following planting, keep in a light and warm place and water freely from the time growth is evident until the foliage dies naturally in the autumn. Then, the soil must remain bone dry until the following year. When flowers appear it will be a signal that feeding with weak liquid fertilizer should begin.

Although frequent potting on is not needed it will benefit the plants to topdress them with new mixture every year. Every four years the bulbs should be repotted and can be divided at the same time to produce new plants.

To encourage bloom:
Observe winter rest period.

Stanhopea wardii

- **Moderate shade**
- **Temp: 10-13°C (50-55°F) min.**
- **Evergreen/dry rest**

In common with the other species, *Stanhopea wardii* produces a 30-38cm (12-15in) broad, leathery leaf from the top of an oval pseudobulb. The flower spike, when it has emerged from the plant container, carries three to nine flowers in late summer. The buds develop very quickly and the flowers, up to 10cm (4in) across when fully open, vary from pale lemon to orange, dotted with brownish-purple, with a large blotch of the same colour on each side of the lip.

Stanhopeas are among the easiest orchids to grow, requiring the conditions of the cool to intermediate house with moderate shade and moisture at the roots at all times. They should be grown in baskets or in purpose-made pots that have holes in the walls and base to prevent the flowers being trapped within the container. A large plant will bloom freely; the spikes open in succession.

To encourage bloom:
Keep moist while active. 136▸

Stephanotis floribunda

(Madagascar jasmine)

- **Good light**
- **Temp: 13-21°C (55-70°F)**
- **Keep moist; dry in winter**

Stephanotis will quickly fill its allotted space if given a free root run. Indoors, it requires a framework around which growth can be trained. Keep on the dry side in winter, and in the lightest possible location at all times, although avoiding direct summer sunshine.

The green, leathery leaves are evergreen and the flowers appear during the summer months. The white tubular flowers are produced in clusters of five or more and have the most overpowering scent.

Grow stephanotis in a loam-based mixture and repot into a slightly larger container every year. Feed with a standard liquid fertilizer every two weeks during the spring and summer and keep the soil and surroundings moist.

Pollinated flowers will occasionally result in large seedpods forming – these should be allowed to burst open before seed is removed and sown. New plants can also be grown from tip cuttings taken in spring.

To encourage bloom:
Keep in stable conditions. 141▸

Strelitzia reginae

(Bird of paradise flower)

- **Sunny location**
- **Temp: 13-24°C (55-75°F)**
- **Keep moist; dry in winter**

This spectacular plant is suitable only where space is adequate; it grows to about 90-120cm (3-4ft) tall when confined to a pot and needs a 30cm (12in) pot when mature. It can be grown from seed but development is painfully slow; from sowing the seed to the production of flowers can be a period of five to ten years. But, if one is patient, the blue and orange flowers are quite a spectacle when they do appear, and have a very long life.

Full sunlight is essential, and plants need potting on when they have filled their existing pots with roots; use loam-based potting mixture at all stages of potting. Feeding is not desperately important and plants will tolerate long periods of draught without appearing to suffer undue harm.

Old clumps can be divided and the sections potted separately. These should flower after two to three years.

To encourage bloom:
Do not disturb mature flowering plants. Grow in sun. 139▸

Streptocarpus hybrids

(Cape primrose; Cape cowslip)

- **Good light**
- **Temp: 16-21°C (60-70°F)**
- **Do not overwater**

In recent years, as with many other more common indoor plants, we have seen considerable improvement in the types of streptocarpus that are being offered for sale. Besides the more usual blue colouring of the variety 'Constant Nymph', there are now white, pink, red and purple shades available.

In culture they are all very similar, and require a light airy location at moderate temperatures to succeed. Place in good light with some protection from direct sunlight, and temperatures in the range 16-21°C (60-70°F). Feed every two weeks during the growing season with a high-phosphate fertilizer. Excessive watering can be damaging, so it is best to water the plant well and allow it to dry before repeating, bearing in mind that plants need much less water and no feed in winter.

New plants are raised by cutting leaves into 10cm (4in) sections and placing them in fresh peat at not less than 18°C (65°F).

To encourage bloom:
Remove seedpods as they form. 139▸

Thunbergia alata

(Black-eyed Susan vine; Clock vine)

- **Sunny location**
- **Temp: 13-18°C (55-65°F)**
- **Keep moist; dry in winter**

The triangular green leaves of this plant sprout from wiry stems that twine around any form of support within reach. Throughout the summer this rather plain foliage backdrop is adorned with striking bright orange flowers each with a jet black centre – hence its apt common name of Black-eyed Susan vine.

Offer a light window location and modest temperature, and feed regularly once the plants have started to grow. For the vigorous twining growth it is essential to provide a framework to which new growth can be attached or allowed to twine naturally around. When potting on use a loam-based potting mixture.

It is best to treat this plant as an annual and raise new plants from seed sown in spring.

To encourage bloom:
Provide plants with plenty of light and sunshine. Pick off flowers as they fade to promote further bloom. 138▸

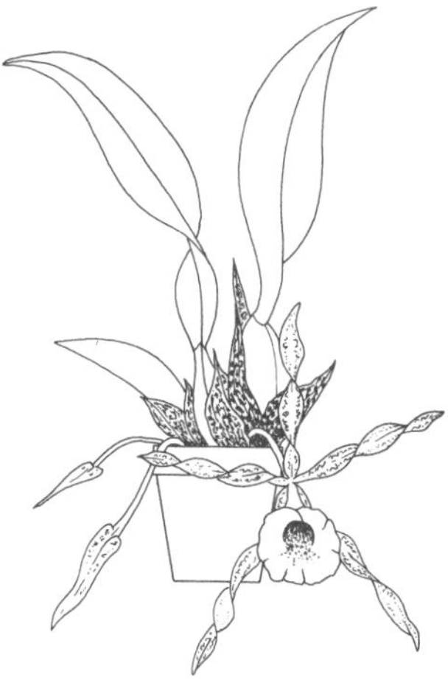

Tillandsia cyanea

(Pink quill)

- **Good light**
- **Temp: 16-21°C (60-70°F)**
- **Water moderately**

From a compact rosette of thin green leaves, *T. cyanea* will in time produce one of the most spectacular of flowering bracts, similar in shape to the cuttle fish. The bract emerges from among the leaves and eventually attains a size of about 15 by 7.5cm (6 by 3in). An added bonus is the appearance of brilliant violet-blue flowers along the margin of the bract over a period of several weeks. As one flower dies so another takes its place.

Avoid getting the soil too wet, and never be tempted to pot plants into large containers, as they will be very much happier in smaller pots in free-draining potting mixture. Use a conventional houseplant mix to which chopped pine needles have been added – the latter will keep the mixture open and prevent sodden conditions. Feeding is not important.

To encourage bloom:
Keep warm and humid.

Trichopilia tortilis

(Corkscrew orchid)

- **Shade during summer**
- **Temp: 10-13°C (50-55°F) min.**
- **Evergreen/semi-rest**

About 30 species of *Trichopilia* are known, although only a few of these are available to growers today. Despite this, they remain very popular, partly because they are not difficult to cultivate and also because of their very showy flowers, which are large in comparison with the size of the plant. The plants are epiphytic and are found mainly in S. America.

The plants, which never grow very tall, develop flattened pseudobulbs that may be rounded or elongated, and a solitary leathery leaf. Intermediate house conditions suit them well, with good shade during the summer months. The plants benefit from generous moisture at the root in full growth. After flowering, these orchids should be allowed a period of semi-rest.

This plant carries a single flower, up to 13cm (5in) across, on a pendent spike. The sepals and petals, which are narrow and twisted throughout their length, are brown, bordered by yellow-green.

To encourage bloom:
Keep moist at roots while active. 141▶

Tulipa

(Tulip)

- **Good light**
- **Temp: 10-16°C (50-60°F)**
- **Keep moist**

Possibly the most colourful of all the spring bulbs, tulips can also be grown successfully indoors for that winter splash of colour. When selecting, choose only the finest quality bulbs if you wish to obtain the best results. Also, it is wise to choose the varieties that are normally recommended for rockeries, as these will be shorter and more appropriate for indoor decoration. Among the rockery varieties there are many fascinating colours, some with the added benefit of attractive foliage.

Plant the bulbs in shallow pans in a fibrous mixture in the autumn and keep them in a cool dark place. Just the tips of the bulbs should be visible above the moistened bulb fibre. When the developing leaves are about 7.5cm (3in) tall transfer the container to a cool light place. When flower buds are just evident, the plants can be transferred to a slightly warmer place, but high temperatures must be avoided.

To encourage bloom:
Grow cool and dark at first. 140▸

Vallota speciosa

(Scarborough lily)

- **Sunny location**
- **Temp: 13-18°C (55-65°F)**
- **Keep moist**

Given reasonable light, moderate temperature, and care to prevent the potting mixture becoming excessively wet, these attractive plants will go on for years with few problems. The bulbous plants have green strap-shaped leaves and attractive scarlet flowers borne on stems about 60cm (2ft) in height.

New plants can be raised from seed or, perhaps more easily, from offsets that form around the base of the parent bulb. The offsets, which are very small, should be removed in the autumn for planting in a group in a shallow pan of peaty mixture. They do not need frequent repotting.

Unlike many bulbs, a resting period is not required, so the mixture – a rich, loam-based one is best – should be kept moist throughout the year. However, at no time should it become excessively wet.

To encourage bloom:
Provide plenty of sunshine. 140▸

Vanda suavis

- **Sunny conditions**
- **Temp: 18°C (65°F) min.**
- **Evergreen/semi-rest**

Coming from Java and Bali, this free-flowering strap-leaved epiphyte bears colourful flowers in autumn and early winter. The stems are densely leafy with curving leaves about 25cm (10in) long and 2.5cm (1in) wide. Flower spikes are horizontal, shorter than the leaves and carry five to ten flowers that vary in shape and colour. Typically they have whitish-yellow sepals and petals barred or spotted with red-brown, usually flushed with pale magenta near the base. The fragrant waxy flowers are about 7.5cm (3in) across. This vanda is moderately easy to coax into bloom in warm sunny conditions, although it should not be attempted by beginners. A well-grown plant can reach to a considerable height and in full leaf is a grand sight. It is also found under the name of *Vanda tricolor.*

New plants, complete with roots, are occasionally formed around the base of the parent.

To encourage bloom:
Grow in full sunlight. 142

Veltheimia viridifolia

(Forest lily)

- **Good light**
- **Temp: 16-21°C (60-70°F)**
- **Keep moist and fed**

This bulbous plant from South Africa deserves to be more popular than it is at present. Leaves are large and soft green in colour. Its flowers – pink tinged with yellow – appear during the winter months.

Bulbs of *V. viridifolia* should be planted in early autumn to flower in winter. Place the bulbs in a loam-based mixture to which a liberal amount of peat has been added; just cover the bulbs with the mixture, ensuring that the potting is done with some firmness. Keep the soil on the dry side until new growth is under way, then water more liberally. Feed with a standard liquid fertilizer every month when in active growth.

They make good centrepiece plants provided they are given cool and light indoor conditions. During the summer place the plants in an unheated greenhouse until required again in the autumn.

To encourage bloom:
Observe summer rest period.

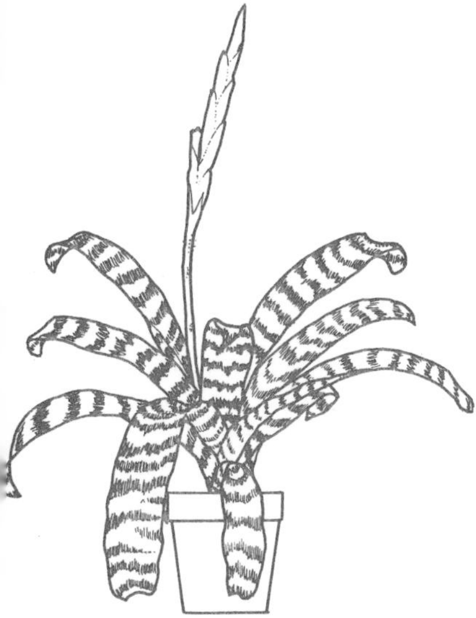

Vriesea splendens

(Flaming sword)

- **Good light; some sunshine**
- **Temp: 16-21°C (60-70°F)**
- **Keep moist; drier in winter**

This plant is a member of the splendid bromeliad family with a typical rosette of overlapping leaves that form a natural urn for holding water. The urn must be kept topped up at all times but needs to be cleaned out and freshly watered.

The broad recurving leaves of *Vriesea splendens* are grey-green in colour with darker bands of brownish purple across the leaf. The flower spike usually develops in the summer and may last for many weeks. The bright red bracts enclosing the short-lived yellow flowers provide the main display.

Grow this plant in a mixture of equal parts of loam-based growing medium and fir bark chips, or use a commercially prepared bromeliad mix. The main rosette flowers only once then dies, but as the plant deteriorates offsets form at the base of the trunk and, once rooted these can be detached and potted separately to provide new plants.

To encourage bloom:
Grow in bright light. 142▸

Zantedeschia rehmannii

(Calla lily; Pink arum; Pink calla; Trumpet lily)

- **Good light**
- **Temp: 10-16°C (50-60°F)**
- **Keep moist; dry in winter**

Frequently seen in flower borders out of doors, this compact arum with attractive leaves and pinkish flowers is also a fine plant for summer flowering indoors. It grows to a height of about 60cm (2ft). Ample water and frequent feeding are essential when plants are in leaf and flower.

In the autumn, when foliage begins to die down naturally, watering should be gradually discontinued until the soil is quite dry. Leave it in this condition until the following early spring. At this time the rhizomes should be repotted into fresh soil with reasonable body to it. A loam-based mixture would be suitable for potting, but a liberal amount of peat should be added.

New plants can be started either from the small offshoots or by dividing the rhizomes when repotting.

To encourage bloom:
Grow in cool conditions when active. Observe rest period from midsummer until late autumn.

Zephyranthes candida

(Swamp lily; Zephyr flower)

- **Good light**
- **Temp: 16-21°C (60-70°F)**
- **Keep moist; dry in winter**

These bulbs are usually planted as outdoor subjects, where they thrive in well-drained loam in full sun. With care, they can be raised indoors, too. This species produces shining white, crocus-like flowers during late summer; pink and orange varieties are also available.

Place 4 or 5 bulbs in a 15cm (6in) pot in spring and cover them with a free-draining potting mix made up of equal parts of loam and peat. Keep the pot in a sunny window and water generously, allowing the soil to dry out between waterings. Feeding is not necessary.

When flowering is over, gradually reduce watering until the leaves die down completely. Store the dry bulbs in a cool, shaded place during the winter months, ready for planting up again the following spring.

Propagate *Zephyranthes* by detaching the offset bulbs that develop beside the main bulb.

To encourage bloom:
Provide bright conditions. 143▸

Zygopetalum intermedium

- **Good light**
- **Temp: 13°C (55°F) min.**
- **Evergreen/dry rest**

This genus comprises 20 species, most of which come from Brazil. They are mainly terrestrial, producing rounded pseudobulbs with long but fairly narrow leaves.

These are plants for the intermediate house and require good light, with plenty of moisture at the root when in full growth. Air movement around the plant in conditions of high humidity is very important, otherwise the leaves soon become badly spotted; they should never be sprayed.

This plant produces an upright flower spike, 45-60cm (18-24in) in height, from inside the first leaves of a new growth. The spike bears four to eight flowers, each 7.5cm (3in) across. The sepals and petals are of equal size, and bright green blotched with brown. The lip, in contrast, is broad, flat and heavily lined with purple. These heavily scented flowers last for four or five weeks during the winter months.

To encourage bloom:
Keep moist at root. 144▸

Index to Common Names

African violet 147
Alpine violet 58
Amaryllis 88
Amazonian zebra plant 19
Amazon lily 64
Angelwing begonia 27
Arabian violet 82
Aztec lily 151

Baby pepper 146
Baby primrose 127
Ball cactus 120
Basket vine 20
Bellflower 17, 49
Bird of paradise flower 152
Black-eyed Susan vine 153
Bleeding heart vine 53
Bloodberry 146
Blood flower 86
Blood lily 86
Bottlebrush 32
Brazilian plume 93
Bush violet 30
Busy Lizzie 92
Butterfly orchid 122

Calamondin orange 53
Calla lily 157
Candy corn plant 116
Cape cowslip 153
Cape jasmine 84
Cape primrose 153
Cardinal flower 146
Catharine wheel 86
Chenille plant 18
Cherry pie 87
Chilean bellflower 113
Chin cactus 85
Chinese hibiscus 88
Chinese rose 88
Christmas cactus 148
Christmas flower 82
Cigar flower 58
Clock vine 153
Clown orchid 121
Cob cactus 114
Cockleshell orchid 62
Cockscomb 51
Comet orchid 22
Common allamanda 21
Common camellia 32, 37
Common hydrangea 91
Common lantana 96
Copihue 113
Coralberry 24
Corkscrew orchid 154
Corn lily 92
Corsage flower 50
Cradle orchid 22
Crimson bottlebrush 32
Crown cactus 145
Crown of thorns 81
Cupid's bower 18

Dancing doll orchid 122
Desert rose 19
Dwarf pomegranate 145

Easter cactus 148
Egyptian star cluster 126
Egyptian star flower 126

Exotic brush 20
Eyelash begonia 26

Fairy primrose 127
Falling stars 49
Firecracker flower 57, 58
Firecracker plant 116
Firecracker vine 116
Flame of the woods 93
Flame violet 63
Flaming Katy 94
Flamingo flower 23
Flamingo lily 23
Flaming sword 157
Florist's mum 52
Flowering maple 17
Forest lily 156
Foxtails 18
French heather 64

Geranium 125
German violet 82
Glory bower 53
Glory lily 84
Gloxinia 149
Golden-rayed lily 113
Golden trumpet 21
Goldfish plant 91
Goldfish vine 55, 56
Grass lily 92

Heath 64
Heliotrope 87
Hot water plant 18
House hydrangea 91
Hyacinth 90

Impala lily 19
Indian azalea 25
Indian jasmine 93
Italian bellflower 49

Jacobean lily 151
Jade plant 56
Jasmine plant 29
Jerusalem cherry 150

Kaffir lily 54
Kahili ginger 86
Kangaroo thorn 17
King's crown 93

Lace flower 63
Lady of the night 30
Lady's eardrops 83
Lady's slipper 123
Lipstick vine 20
Living stone 114
Love plant 117

Madagascar jasmine 152
Madagascar periwinkle 50
Mexican cigar plant 58
Miniature wax plant 89
Moth orchid 126

Oilcloth flower 23
Oleander 119
Orange star 85
Orchid cactus 62
Ornamental chilli 49

Painter's palette 23
Pansy orchid 117, 118
Paper flower 29
Passion flower 124
Patience plant 92
Patient Lucy 92
Peace lily 150
Peanut cactus 51
Persian violet 82
Pigtail plant 23
Pink allamande 60
Pink arum 157
Pink calla 157
Pink jasmine 94
Pink quill 154
Plume celosia 51
Pocketbook plant 31
Poinsettia 82
Poor man's orchid 58
Porcelain flower 89
Pouch flower 31
Prince of Wales' feathers 51

Queen of the bromeliads 19

Rainbow cactus 61
Red ginger 21
Red hot cat's tail 18
Red pepper 49
Rose bay 119
Rose grape 117
Rose mallow 88
Rose pin cushion 115
Rouge plant 146

Saffron spike 24
Sand dollar cactus 25
Scarborough lily 155
Scarlet plume 81
Scarlet star 85
Sea urchin cactus 25, 61
Shooting star 58
Shrimp plant 28
Shrub verbena 96
Silver vase 20
Slipper flower 31
Slipper orchid 123
Slipperwort 31
Snap weed 92
Snowball flower 91
Spanish shawl 147
Spathe flower 150
Spear flower 24
Star-of-Bethlehem 49
Stone face 114
Sultana 92
Swamp lily 158

Tailflower 23
Tea plant 32, 37
Temple bells 149
Thistle globe 61
Tiger orchid 121
Tom Thumb 94
Touch-me-not 92
Trailing campanula 49
Tree gloxinia 95
Trompetilla 29
Trumpet lily 157
Tulip 155
Tulip orchid 22

Urn plant 20

Vase plant 20

Wattle 17
Wax begonia 27
Wax plant 89, 90
Wax vine 89
White flag 150
White sails 150
Winter cherry 150

Yellow sage 96

Zebra plant 24
Zephyr flower 158

Picture Credits

The publishers wish to thank the following photographers and agencies who have supplied photographs for this book. Photographs have been credited by page number and position on the page: (B) Bottom, (T) Top, (C) Centre, (BL) Bottom left, etc.

A–Z Botanical Collection: 10(T), 13(B), 34(BL), 138(L), 138–9(B), 141(B)
Pat Brindley: 42(BL), 44(BL), 79(B), 110(B), 111
Peter Chapman: 46, 70(BL), 100(T), 100–101(B), 106
Eric Crichton: Back endpaper, 8, 9, 12, 13(T), 14, 15, 16(T), 33, 34(T), 36, 37(T), 38, 42(T), 43, 44(T), 47, 48(BL), 65, 66(TL), 66–7(B), 68(TL), 72(B), 74(B), 75(B), 76(BL), 77, 79(TL), 80, 97, 98(B), 101(T), 102, 103(B), 104(T), 105(T), 107, 109, 112, 129(T), 134(T), 136, 137, 140(T), 141, 142(B), 144
Derek Fell: 139(T)
Kees Hageman: 68(BL)
B. J. van der Lans: 11(B), 78, 143
Gordon Rowley: 11
Daan Smit: Front endpaper, Title page, 39, 105(BR), 134(B), 140(BL)
Harry Smith Photograph Collection: Half title page, 10(B), 72(T), 75(T), 79(TR), 98(T), 108(BL), 129(BR), 142(T)
Michael Warren: 41(B), 99, 103(T)

PRINTED IN BELGIUM BY proost INTERNATIONAL BOOK PRODUCTION